THE
WONDERFUL WORLD
OF
FREEZER COOKING

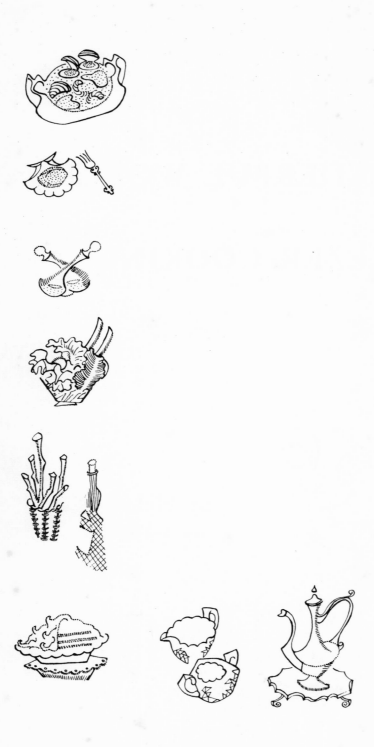

THE
WONDERFUL WORLD
OF
FREEZER COOKING

by Helen Quat

(who also did the drawings)

New York: Hearthside Press

Dedication

To Joanie and Danny, who tasted and tested, and to my husband, Leon, who now regards himself as a "man for all seasonings."

TABLE OF CONTENTS

Introduction,   10
Useful Information,   13
Hors D'oeuvres,   23
Bread,   41
Soup,   51
Meat,   63
Poultry,   91
Fish,   109
Vegetables and Grains,   125
Desserts,   143
Stock Piling and Garnishes,   183
Party Menus,   201
Index,   216

Thank you

To all my friends who made suggestions and ate my experiments, especially Marion Abrams, Mary Evans, Betty Gould, Janet Karson, Bebe Kroll, Paul Petroff, and Esther Shatter.

introduction

To the hostess who wants
to enjoy her own parties . . . and family meals too

I am sure you feel about entertaining as I do. You enjoy your friends. You like to feed them—superbly—and be with them too. You want your parties to be shining and warm and topnotch. You want to look and feel that way too. (And I don't mean your nose is shining or that your warmth is from a hot stove.)

These are the qualities I've aimed at, too, encouraged by a husband who loves people and giving parties and blessed with recollections of my mother's fabulous parties where the food smelled divine and so did she—as she floated in Caron's "Bellodgia."

How is it possible to cook and serve your guests splendiferous food (and I think they are entitled to more than a good home-cooked Monday night meal), and still have energy left to be at the party?

It took me a long time to find the answer. Even when the food was a success, the timing seemed so difficult. Dinner would be late and our guests drank too many cocktails while I toiled in a frenzy in the kitchen.

Gradually, I caught on to planning and cooking ahead. So—for several days in advance of each party, there was a mad scramble of marketing, cooking, and shoving things around in the refrigerator to make room for that large casserole and several chiffon pies.

Then I discovered the wonderful world of freezer cooking. New vistas opened up for joy in the role of a hostess.

Undaunted by gourmet skeptics disdainful of frozen cookery, I experimented and found that there were many wonderful dishes you could cook and store in your freezer, weeks ahead of your party. And when I say freezer, I mean any type, from the walk-in kind to the small compartment at the top or bottom of a refrigerator.

A NEW SYSTEM OF PARTY GIVING

The system is simple. As soon as the invitations are out, you dream up your menu, cook it, and store it in the freezer. Then you forget about the party until the day before.

The day before: You can have your hair done if, like mine, it always looks better the next day, check and restock liquors and soda, clean coat closet of miscellaneous rubbers, ice skates, and torn sweaters, and do any non-freezable preparation—a few small things like salad dressing, raw or marinated vegetables, cocktail dips, etc. That evening, following the recipe, you can transfer from the freezer to the refrigerator whatever needs slow thawing, then you can go to the movies.

The morning of the party: You market for fresh salad greens and fresh flowers too, while you're at it. You wash and tear up the greens, wrap them in a dish towel, and store in the refrigerator, all ready to be tossed. You arrange the flowers, make extra ice cubes to store in the freezer, put cigarettes and candy in appropriate places, put soda and ginger ale on ice, set the table, and relax.

About three hours before guests are due, remove from the freezer the food to be heated. This is to make sure you don't forget a dish tucked away behind that big turkey you're saving for another occasion. Also to start food thawing and to give you a chance to wash and put away the freezer containers. Now your kitchen is spotless. The food is all lined up, ready to heat, the salad is waiting to be tossed, and you've got everything under control.

A little while before you dress is the usual time to start the frozen food slowly heating, either in the oven or double boiler. Reheating schedules are included in my recipes, but in most cases a little more (not less) won't hurt anything. So—have a good soak in the tub while your children are eating their individual meat loaves out of the foil pan in which you've frozen and baked them. (For just such an occasion, to make less preparation time and clean-up mess).

I assume, in the meantime, your husband is arranging the bar, you having made provisions for enough ice cubes, glasses, and lemon peel.

Five minutes before zero, put out the cold hors d'oeuvres, have the oven hot so the other hors d'oeuvres can be popped in as soon as the doorbell rings.

You are on schedule! Your automatic timer reminds you when it's time to remove the hot puffs or devilled crabmeat and thus to serve your first course.

When your guests are on their second drink, that's the time to heat up the frozen vegetables, mix them with the toasted almonds or sautéed mushrooms taken from your freezer, toss the salad, pour the water, and set out the piping hot food. The dessert is waiting either in the refrigerator, the freezer, or on the counter, you plug in the automatic coffee pot—and wasn't it all easy?

Have a great time!

Helen Quat

P.S. Family meals from the freezer can be like parties too.

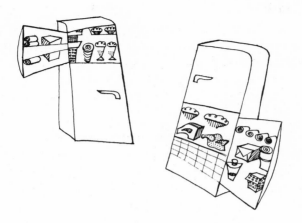

useful information

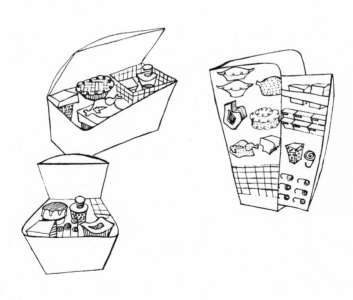

1

ABOUT WHAT TO FREEZE

The recipes in this book include hot and cold appetizers, soups, breads, meat, fish, poultry, vegetables, rice and pasta dishes, and desserts. All of them can be cooked, frozen and thawed, or reheated. All have been guest-tested.

I've even won over some diehard guests who were ready to throw out the freezer with the dishwater, because it didn't transform every bit of leftover roast or stew. You can't toss *everything* into the freezer and expect fabulous results. A broiled chicken, reheated, will be dry on the inside and soggy on the outside. A rather dry slice of roast beef or turkey won't taste any better, unless of course, you combine it with other ingredients to create a new dish. In that case, you'd be using your head and your freezer properly.

In other words, if you think of your freezer only as a storage place for leftovers, your food will taste leftover. But if you prepare your dishes specially for the freezer, part of the cooking is done before and the rest after. Undercook before freezing to avoid overcooking in reheating.

ABOUT VEGETABLES AND SALADS

Not many vegetable recipes are included, because freshly cooked vegetables are so good and take so short a time to prepare. However, with toasted almonds, grated coconut or other embellishments from your freezer (see Chapter 10), you can fancy up fresh or commercially frozen vegetables so that they become irresistible.

Very often, a large green salad with tasty additions replaces a vegetable on my menu; it is texturally more refreshing. My favorite ingredients besides the inevitable lettuce (make it Boston if you can), are spinach leaves, escarole, dandelion, endive cut in long thin strips, slices of raw marinated zucchini, red onion rings, raw cauliflower, mushrooms, cucumbers, cooked beets and artichoke hearts (canned or frozen, first marinated in oil and vinegar), and chopped cooked eggplant, also soaked in oil and vinegar. Don't forget chopped fresh herbs like basil, tarragon, or dill, dried caraway or dill seed, crumbled Roquefort cheese, garlic croutons, freshly ground pepper, a good light oil and wine vinegar, or sometimes a dressing made with sour cream. The list could go on and on. The only thing I would not include would be fresh, farm-grown tomatoes. They should be served alone with chopped fresh basil and maybe a pinch of salt.

cool cooked food in ice water

ABOUT COOLING

Cooling quickly is very important to preserve flavor and quality. Transfer food from hot pot to another pot or bowl. Cover it and submerge in a pan of iced water. Pack in container and freeze.

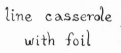

line casserole with foil

ABOUT HEATING

Sit freezer container in hot water to facilitate removal of frozen block. Heat over boiling water, over low direct heat, or in oven. Occasionally, break up frozen block with heavy fork or knife, to hasten thawing.

Many dishes can be frozen in the casserole they were baked in and then reheated in the same dish. Or the casserole can be lined with foil, the food frozen in it, then removed, wrapped and stored in freezer. Reheat in same casserole. Baking dishes such as pyrex, enamelled steel or iron, or the new Corning Ware can go directly from the freezer into the hot oven. It is wiser, however, when using earthenware, to thaw it for an hour at room temperature or to put it into the cold oven before bringing it up to cooking temperature.

If you haven't a large double boiler, improvise with a smaller pot inside a larger pot. When cooking over direct heat, a flame-tamer or similar metal plate with some holes in it, placed between the pot and the flame, will prevent the food at the bottom from cooking too fast before the top is hot.

flame-tamer

The instructions given in my recipes for reheating are from the frozen state unless otherwise indicated. However, some foods, such as soups, stews and some vegetables, can be thawed at room temperature for several hours and the reheating time shortened.

ABOUT QUICK-FREEZING

Place cooled container in quick-freeze compartment or against coils of chest or upright freezer. In refrigerator-freezers, turn temperature control to coldest point to hasten freezing action.

ABOUT PACKAGING

Invest in polyethylene containers or glass freezer jars. They can be washed thoroughly and used indefinitely. Aluminum foil is great for wrapping. It conforms to any shape and serves as a cover without any taping or tying. And if you're careful with it, you can re-use it. Saran wrap has the same qualities. Of course you'll need polyethylene bags, too, with wire twistems for fastening. Small jelly jars with covers are useful for storing 4 or 5 egg whites, chopped nuts, etc. Coffee and shortening cans are fine too if cleaned well first. Seal lids with tape.

If you are reduced to using old glass jars that you've been saving for years, be prepared to allow hours of thawing time because you can't remove the frozen contents through the small opening. Also be sure to leave at least an inch of expansion room on top. If you don't, you'll end up with chicken soup and ground glass.

Labels are important. You think you'll remember, but you don't always. Freezer tape is easy to write on with a soft dark pencil.

Use small size containers wherever possible, because the food thaws more quickly. If you do use gallon size containers, fill halfway, lay a double thickness of freezer paper on surface and fill remaining half. When heating, separate blocks at division.

freeze
on flat surface

Some foods should be frozen on a flat surface till solid, and then packaged in a large container or bag. A flat surface could be a tray, baking sheet, pie plate, or cardboard covered with aluminum foil. Hard to handle food like Quiche Lorraine is easier to freeze unwrapped and packaged when solidly frozen. Pies can be covered with a paper pie plate and then wrapped in foil or placed in a plastic bag.

Foods can be frozen in the casseroles they were baked in and tightly covered with the lid or aluminum foil. Seal the sides with tape. If you want the casserole for another purpose you can remove the food when it is solidly frozen and wrap it in a moistureproof covering. To remove frozen block, set casserole in hot water for a minute, loosen sides with a knife, and invert onto freezer wrapping and wrap. Return to same size casserole for reheating.

seal with tape

ABOUT COOKING FROZEN RAW MEAT

The enemy of frozen meat is textural breakdown resulting in loss of juices. To avoid this:

(1) Wrap carefully in moisture- and vapor-proof material.

(2) Freeze quickly and maintain a constant zero-or-below freezer temperature.

(3) Cook the meat while still frozen.

Never thaw at room temperature or the lovely juices will go down the drain.

If you prefer to thaw before cooking, place the meat, still wrapped, in the refrigerator, and be patient. A 3-rib roast beef will take about 2 days to thaw.

COOKING TIMES

Allow about twice the cooking time for frozen meat. A 6-pound, 2-inch steak, to be served rare, will take 35 to 40 minutes to broil and a standing rib roast needs 43 minutes per pound instead of 18.

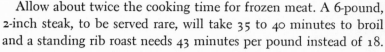

Broiling: Place meat about 2" further from heat than normally until thawed. Then season and place closer to heat.

timer

Roasting: Use a low temperature and insert a meat thermometer after it has cooked for half the planned time. Roast until desired temperature is reached.

Braising or stewing: Cooking time is about the same as for fresh or thawed meats because steam or liquid thaws more quickly.

If you plan to bread, stuff or deep-fry the meat, thaw it first.

Frozen ground meat loses more juice and textural quality when thawed or cooked than solid meat. It does better in meat balls, spaghetti sauce or meat balls than in hamburgers. If you do want hamburger available at a moment's notice, even if it's not the greatest, season the meat with pepper and garlic or onion powder, omitting salt (which may cause rancidity in ground meat) and freeze in patties individually wrapped or packed in layers with a separation of 2 thicknesses of freezer paper or foil. Broil while still frozen. Do not thaw first or try to pan-broil or the outside will be done before the inside.

separate patties
with foil or paper

Poultry is another matter. It should be thawed slowly before cooking, except for soup fowl, which can thaw in the soup as it cooks. Poultry or meat which had been frozen before cooking can be refrozen after it is cooked.

ABOUT HOW LONG TO STORE

meat
thermometer

Don't be a hoarder. Eat your food and keep your inventory changing. A month's storage is a safe average for cooked foods. Some things like soup stock or meat or poultry in lots of liquid will retain quality after 6 months' storage while others like sliced roasted meat or poultry should be kept no longer than 2 weeks.

ABOUT WHAT NOT TO FREEZE

do not freeze

POSITIVELY NOT

Hard-cooked egg white becomes hard and rubbery (unless chopped very fine and used in very small proportion of dish, such as in chopped liver).

Aspics, gelatin salads or desserts get rubbery and weepy.

Raw salad ingredients, such as cucumbers, radishes, celery, tomato, lettuce and other greens: Crispness is lost. Exception— green pepper.

Cooked potatoes or rice frozen in liquid, like soups or stews become mealy and soggy and taste like left-overs.

Mayonnaise curdles (unless in very small ratio to other ingredients).

Stuffing in cooked or raw poultry: Bacteria growth is rapid while roasting because the stuffing is luke-warm for so long before the heat penetrates through the bird.

Broiled or quickly cooked meats or fish: Obviously these would be overcooked if you froze them after cooking and then tried to reheat them. The same rule would apply to rare roasts.

Left-over cooked food: Food that has been cooked, frozen and reheated should not be refrozen, since in the second reheating it will be overcooked. Also while it sits in the serving dish waiting to be eaten and then gets cooled to go back in the freezer, the bacteria flourishes in the luke-warm temperature.

Clear soups, stock and sauce are the one exception, if they are cooled quickly.

WHY BOTHER?

Garden-grown produce: If you have a farm-sized garden, the freezer may be needed for your harvest but I do not freeze garden crops for 2 reasons: (1) The flavor and texture of freshly picked produce are superior to that of frozen vegetables and fruits. (2) The blanching process (immersing in boiling water and quickly cooling in ice water, both for exactly the right time) is a nuisance. And the end result can never be as good as the commercially frozen vegetables and fruits, which are processed in ways you can't duplicate.

My one exception is to freeze herbs. You can't use them up during the growing season. Except for parsley, you can't buy them fresh or frozen, and if you don't require crispness and use herbs only to flavor cooking, they're fine. And easy. No blanching, just wash, drain, dry well and pack.

mint

tarragon

basil

dill

parsley

ABOUT COOKING AND SERVING IN QUANTITY

Your freezer is a great asset when you're expecting many people. You'll be able to get the bulk of the preparation done ahead of time and stored in the freezer, so that neither you nor your refrigerator are ready to burst when The Day comes.

To cook in quantity, all you need is an ability to multiply (or a husband who can), and several large pots and gallon-size freezer containers. Don't try to cook everything in one gigantic pot (except soup). Rather, multiply your recipe to the total quantity needed and then divide it between your 4 burners and 4 pots. This way the food is more manageable, the stirring is easier, the cooking temperature is more uniform and the tasting is more accurate.

Then, after you have cooled the food quickly over ice, place it in gallon containers, in two layers, with a double thickness of foil or freezer paper between. This will prevent the food from freezing into gallon chunks. You will be able to separate the layers at the division and so shorten the thawing or heating time.

fill container half-way — place foil or paper on surface

On the day of the party, partially thaw the food to be heated at room temperature. Then you can carefully break it up into smaller divisions, so that the reheating will be more uniform throughout. Do not try to reheat in too large a pot, because the bottom will be overcooked before the top is even warm. Rather, heat in several heavy pots over a very low heat or in a double boiler, until completely heated. Then, if you like you can transfer it all to one enormous pot.

Plan a menu which uses the whole stove. If you are serving a baked side dish, your oven will be too full for the main dish. So plan to reheat your meat on a top burner. The oven casseroles can go right to the table (buffet, I'm assuming) and will stay hot. Transfer the food from the top burner pots to chafing dishes or serving dishes kept warm on an electric hot tray.

For dessert, try to plan one which can be served from the freezer, because you probably won't have room to thaw it in the refrigerator.

I've found it helpful to write down (for myself or anyone I'm having in to help) the menu and exact procedures to follow: What time the casserole goes in the oven, at what temperature, when to add the sherry, when to unmold the mousse, etc. Also, writing down the menu reminds you to add to the salad those red onion rings which you've carefully sliced and placed somewhere deep in the refrigerator.

*

For those who would like to cook some recipes without freezing the end product, the asterisk indicates the point at which you may continue preparation for immediate service, following the instructions also marked with an asterisk at the end of each recipe.

In a few dessert recipes, this symbol has been omitted because these dishes must be frozen.

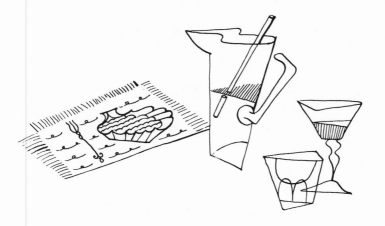

hors d'oeuvres

2

CLAM BEIGNETS
(36 puffs)

Minced clams, 10-oz. can
Butter, 4 tablespoons
Flour, ¾ cup
Eggs, 2
Salt, 1 teaspoon

Black pepper, ⅛ teaspoon
Dill seed, crushed, ¼ teaspoon
Thyme, ⅛ teaspoon
Chives, chopped, ½ teaspoon

1. Drain clams: reserve ½ cup liquor. Heat butter with clam liquor. As soon as it boils, pour in flour. Stir vigorously with a wooden spoon over low heat until mixture leaves the sides of the pan and forms a smooth ball.

2. Transfer to mixing bowl. Beat in eggs, 1 at a time, with clams and seasonings.

3. Grease baking pan. Drop batter by ½ teaspoons onto pan. Bake at 400° F. for 20 minutes, until golden brown.* Remove and cool. Freeze on flat surface. When firm, pack in plastic bag or container.

Serving day: Place frozen on cooky sheet and heat at 350° F. for 10 to 15 minutes.

Ready to serve without freezing.

CLAM BROTH PUFFS
(about 60 puffs)

Clam broth, 1 cup
(or liquid drained from
10½-oz. can of clams
plus 1 cup water)
Butter, ½ cup

Flour, 1 cup
Eggs, 5 at room temperature
Milk, ½ teaspoon
Clam or Crabmeat Filling
(recipes follow)

1. Heat liquid in saucepan. Add butter and bring to a boil. Add flour all at once and stir vigorously with a wooden spoon over low heat until mixture leaves the sides of the pan and forms a smooth ball.

2. Transfer to mixing bowl. Add 4 eggs, one at a time, beating thoroughly after each addition until thick dough is formed.

3. Place level teaspoons of batter on ungreased baking sheet about 1" apart. Brush tops with remaining egg beaten with milk. Bake at 400° F. for 10 minutes. Reduce heat to 300° F. without opening oven door and bake for 20 to 25 minutes.

4. Cool, cut in half and fill with desired filling. Replace tops.* Freeze on flat tray. When firm, pack in plastic bag or container.

Serving day: Heat at 400° F. for 15 minutes.

*Ready to serve without freezing.

mixture leaves the sides of the pan and forms a ball

CLAM FILLING FOR PUFFS

(3 cups)

Minced clams, 3 cans (each 10½ ounces)
Chive cheese, 6 3-ounce packages

Tabasco, 6 dashes
Pepper, ½ teaspoon
Lawry seasoned salt, 1 teaspoon

Drain clams. Soften cheese. Combine all ingredients and mix thoroughly.

CRABMEAT FILLING FOR PUFFS

(3 cups)

Crabmeat, cooked or canned, 3 cups
Cream cheese, 3 3-ounce packages, softened

Salt, 1½ teaspoons
Pepper, 1 teaspoon
Minced chives, 1½ teaspoons
Dill seed, 1½ teaspoons

Pick over crabmeat and shred finely. Combine all ingredients and mix thoroughly.

CHOPPED CHICKEN LIVER

(3 cups makes 5 or 6 dozen canapés)

Chicken fat, 3 tablespoons	Salt, 1 teaspoon
Onions, sliced, 3	Pepper, ½ teaspoon
Chicken livers, 1 pound	Dill seed, 1 teaspoon
Eggs, hard-cooked, 4	

Heat fat in frying pan and sauté onions till golden. Lift out with slotted spoon. Add livers to pan and brown well on both sides. Combine livers, onions, eggs and seasoning and chop coarsely.* Pack in ½-pint containers. Freeze.

Night before serving: Thaw livers in refrigerator for 24 hours.

Or on Serving day: Heat at 300° F. for 20 minutes, occasionally stirring with fork. Chop again when completely thawed. serve cold.

To serve now, chop fine.

CHICKEN LIVER BEIGNETS

(50)

Butter, 4 tablespoons	Black pepper, ¼ teaspoon
Chicken broth, ½ cup	Salt, ½ teaspoon
Flour, ¾ cup	Dill seeds, ½ teaspoon
Eggs, 2	Chopped liver, 1 cup

1. Heat butter with chicken broth. When it reaches the boiling point, pour in flour. Cook over low heat and stir vigorously with a wooden spoon until mixture leaves the sides of the pan and forms a smooth ball.

2. Transfer to mixing bowl. Beat in eggs one at a time. Fold in chopped liver and seasoning.

3. Grease baking sheets. Drop batter by teaspoons on sheets. Bake at 400° F. for 15 minutes or fry in deep fat for 3 or 4 minutes till golden brown.* Remove and cool. Freeze on flat surface. When firm, pack in plastic bag or container.

Serving day: Place frozen beignets on cooky sheet and heat at 350° F. for 20 to 25 minutes.

Ready to serve without freezing.

CHICKEN LIVER PATE WITH COGNAC

(1½ quarts)

Butter or margarine, 1½ cups
Onion, chopped, 1
Chicken livers, cut up, 1 pound
Chicken broth, 2¾ cups
Marsala wine, 2 tablespoons
Paprika, ½ teaspoon
Curry, ½ teaspoon

Salt, ½ teaspoon
Pepper, ⅛ teaspoon
Garlic, crushed, 2 cloves
Cognac, ⅓ cup
Walnuts, coarsely chopped and
    toasted in oven, 1 cup
Gelatin, 2 tablespoons

push pâté
¼ inch away
from sides of
pan

1. Heat 1 cup butter, sauté onion until golden. Add livers and cook for about 10 minutes, stirring occasionally. Add ¾ cup of broth, wine, seasonings and garlic. Cook for 5 minutes.

2. Purée mixture in electric blender. Melt remaining butter and blend into purée with cognac. Stir in walnuts with a fork.

3. Lightly grease 2 shallow 8" x 8" pans.* Pour in pâté and refrigerate for 2 hours or more. When firm, use spatula to push pâté about ¼" away from the 4 sides of pans, to make room for aspic. Place in freezer. When frozen, remove from pans and wrap. Return to freezer.

Night before serving: 1. Soften 1 tablespoon of gelatin in 1 cup of cold broth. Heat, stirring until dissolved. Oil the same 8" x 8" pans and pour in gelatin mixture. Chill until firm.

2. Unwrap the paté and place in pans. Soften remaining table-spoon of gelatin in 1 cup of cold broth. Heat, stirring until dissolved. Pour into ¼" space along the sides of pans. Refrigerate. Unmold to serve. Serve with cocktail size rye bread.

pour aspic into
¼ inch spaces

Note: This can be unmolded 1 or 2 hours before serving, arranged on a platter and refrigerated until time to serve.

> *To serve without freezing, cover bottom of greased pans with aspic and chill until firm. Pour in pâté. When firm, push away from sides of pans and pour in remaining aspic. Refrigerate.*

As an alternate arrangement, after walnuts are stirred in, pack pâté into pint containers and freeze. Thaw in refrigerator overnight. When thawed, shape it with your hands into a pineapple. Decorate with stuffed olive slices and cap with a pineapple top.

HOT FILLED TURNOVERS
(about 80)

Flour, 4½ cups
Salt, ¼ teaspoon
Vegetable shortening, 2 cups
 (1 pound)
Vinegar, ½ cup
Water, ¾ cup

Egg, 1
Cheese or Meat filling
 (recipe follows) or
Chopped Chicken Liver, 4 cups
 (see index)
Butter, melted, 3 tablespoons

1. Mix salt with flour. Cut in shortening. Add vinegar and water gradually and mix in with a fork. Beat egg lightly and stir into dough. Turn out on wax paper and press into a ball. Chill in refrigerator overnight.

2. Cut dough into 4 sections. Roll out 1 at a time, to ⅛" thickness. Cut into 2½" circles, using a glass or cooky cutter.

3. Place 1 teaspoon of filling on half of each piece. Fold over remaining half. Moisten edges with water and press together with tines of a fork. Brush with melted butter.* Freeze on flat tray and pack in a plastic bag or container.

Serving day: Bake at 425° F. for 20 minutes.

 **To serve without freezing, bake as directed.*

cut into circles

place   fold   press   brush with   freeze on
filling   over   with fork   butter   flat surface

CHEESE FILLING FOR TURNOVERS

(4 cups)

Cream cheese, 2 cups (1 pound)
Chive cream cheese, 2 cups
 (1 pound)

Anchovy paste, 1-ounce tube
Heavy cream, 5 tablespoons

Soften cheese. Combine all ingredients and mix thoroughly.

MEAT FILLING FOR TURNOVERS

Butter, 6 tablespoons
Chopped lean beef, 1 pound
Onions, chopped, 2 medium
Scallions, chopped, 2 stalks
Flour, 2 tablespoons
Canned tomatoes, drained and
  crushed, 1 cup

Marsala wine, ¼ cup
Fresh parsley, chopped,
  4 tablespoons
Fresh dill, 4 tablespoons or
  1 teaspoon powdered dill
Salt, 1½ teaspoons
Cayenne, ¼ teaspoon
Paprika, ½ teaspoon

1. Heat 4 tablespoons of butter in skillet. Add meat and cook until brown. Remove meat and grind or chop very fine.

2. Heat remaining butter in skillet and cook onions and scallions until lightly browned. Stir in flour. Add tomatoes and wine and cook until thickened. Stir in parsley, dill, seasoning, and meat. Cool before filling.

TOASTED CARAWAY CHEESE CANAPES

(18 canapés)

Egg, 1
Cream cheese, 4 ounces
Onion, finely chopped, 1
Salt, ½ teaspoon

Pepper, ⅛ teaspoon
Chives, ¼ teaspoon
Cocktail size rye bread, 18 slices
Caraway seeds, 4 teaspoons

1. Beat egg and mix with softened cream cheese, onion, salt, pepper and chives until well blended.

2. Spread mix on bread slices. Sprinkle with caraway seeds.* Freeze on flat surface. When firm, pack in containers with freezer paper between layers. Return to freezer.

Serving day: Broil 4" from flame until brown. Serve hot.

To serve without freezing, broil as directed.

CARAWAY-CHEESE STRAWS
(about 30)

Butter, ½ cup
Cream cheese, 4 ounces
Flour, sifted, 1 cup
Salt, ¼ teaspoon

Egg yolk, 1
Milk, 2 teaspoons
Grated Parmesan cheese, ⅓ cup
Caraway seeds, 2 teaspoons

1. Soften butter and cream cheese and cream together. Blend in flour and salt gradually. Form into a ball. Chill overnight.

2. Divide dough in half. Roll each half into a rectangle about ⅜" thick. Dilute egg yolk with milk and brush on pastry. Sprinkle with grated cheese and caraway seeds. Cut pastry into strips about ¾" x 3".

3. Place on greased cooky sheet. Bake on upper shelf at 450° F. for 8 or 9 minutes.* Cool. Freeze on flat tray. When firm, pack in container and return to freezer.

Serving day: Heat at 350° F. for 5 minutes. Serve hot or warm.
Ready to serve without freezing.

cut into
strips

CURRIED CHEESE BALL OR SLICES
(about 50 slices)

Cream cheese, 8 ounces
Sharp Cheddar cheese, grated,
  8 ounces
Cream cheese with chives,
  3 ounces

Walnuts, chopped, 1 cup
Olives, chopped, 1 teaspoon
Garlic, crushed, 3 cloves
Curry powder, 1 tablespoon

Soften cream cheese and mix well with other ingredients. Form into a ball. Wrap and freeze; or form into two long rolls about 1½" in diameter.* Wrap in foil and freeze.

Serving day: Thaw ball at room temperature and serve with crackers; or thaw rolls at room temperature for 10 minutes and slice about ¼" thick. Serve on crackers.
To serve without freezing, refrigerate until firm.

QUICHE LORRAINE
(1 9" pie or 7 tarts)

PASTRY

Flour, sifted, 1¼ cups
Butter, soft, ½ cup
Egg yolk, 1
Salt, 1 teaspoon

Dry mustard, ½ teaspoon
Paprika, 1 teaspoon
Ice water, 1 tablespoon

1. Put flour into a large bowl, leaving a well in the center. Put butter, egg yolk, and seasoning into the well. With fingers of one hand, work center ingredients into a smooth paste. Gradually work in the flour. Sprinkle with ice water and gather into a ball. Wrap in waxed paper. Chill in refrigerator for 30 minutes.

2. Roll out ⅛" thick on floured board. Line 9" pie plate; or cut into rounds and fit into tart pans. Flute edges and bake at 450° F. for 5 minutes. Cool and put in freezer for 1 hour or longer before filling.

QUICHE FILLING

Butter, 1 tablespoon
Small white onions, finely
  chopped, 2
Cooked ham, shredded, ½ cup
Grated Swiss cheese, 1 cup
Eggs, 4

Cream, 2 cups
Salt, ½ teaspoon
Cayenne, ½ teaspoon
White pepper, ½ teaspoon
Nutmeg, ¼ teaspoon

pie is
ready if
knife comes
out clean

(*Note:* For tarts, cut filling recipe in half.)
  Sauté onions in butter until transparent. Place ham on bottom of frozen pie. Sprinkle cheese and onion on top of ham. Beat eggs, cream, and seasonings and strain over onion-cheese mixture.* Freeze on flat surface. Wrap.

Serving day: Bake on lower shelf at 450° F. for 15 minutes. Reduce heat to 350° F. and bake for 50 minutes on upper shelf or until custard is set. (Test: Insert knife 1" from edge. If it comes out clean, pie is ready.)

> *To serve without freezing, bake now, but reduce
> final baking at 350° F. to 25 minutes.*

SPANAKOPETES
Greek Spinach-Cheese Triangles
(about 35)

Spinach, frozen whole leaf,
10-ounce package or fresh,
1 pound
Olive oil, 3 tablespoons
Onion, finely chopped, 1
Feta cheese (from Greek grocer
or gourmet shop), ½ pound
Pot cheese, 6 ounces
Parsley, chopped, ¼ cup

Dried dill weed, 1 teaspoon
Salt, ½ teaspoon
Pepper, ⅛ teaspoon
Eggs, 3
Corn flake crumbs, ¼ cup
Frozen phyllo sheets, or Fillo-
Strudel (from Greek grocer or
gourmet shop), ½ pound
Butter, ¼ pound

1. Thaw frozen spinach at room temperature (about 3 hours) or wash fresh spinach. Drain very thoroughly and cut up with a scissors. Heat oil and sauté onion until wilted. Add spinach and simmer, stirring occasionally until moisture evaporates.

2. Crumble Feta cheese in a bowl. Blend in pot cheese, parsley, dill, salt and pepper. Beat eggs and mix with cheese. Add spinach mixture and crumbs and blend thoroughly.

3. Thaw phyllo sheets at room temperature just enough to spread sheets out. Cut in thirds. Wrap two-thirds in a towel and refrigerate until needed. Wrap one-third in a dampened towel. Remove 1 sheet at a time to work with.

4. Melt butter. Lay 1 phyllo sheet on wax paper and brush liberally with butter. Fold in the 2 long sides towards the middle, making a strip about 2" wide x 11" long. Brush liberally with butter again.

5. Place 1 tablespoon of spinach-cheese mixture in a bottom corner of strip. Fold pastry (with filling) over, so that the bottom edge meets a side edge and forms a right-angle triangle shape. Continue folding over from side to side into neat triangles until end of strip. Brush finished triangle with butter.

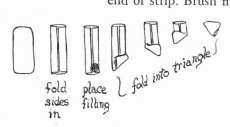

fold
sides
in

place
filling

fold into triangle

6. When refrigerated pastry is needed, remove ½ at a time and wrap in dampened towel. Follow preceding process until all ingredients are used.* Freeze on flat surface. Pack frozen triangles in freezer container or bag and return to freezer.

Serving day: Place triangles on a baking pan (not a cooky sheet because butter drips). Bake at 425° F. for 20 to 25 minutes, turning once, until browned on both sides. Cool 5 minutes before serving.

Serves as an hors d'oeuvres (napkins needed), or as an accompaniment to soup. With Russian cabbage soup, this makes a full meal.

To serve without freezing, bake as directed.

FLAGEOLET OR WHITE BEAN SALAD
(8 to 10 servings—4 cups)

Dry flageolets or dried small white pea beans, 2 cups (1 pound)	Salt, 2 teaspoons
	Onion, 1
	Cloves, 5
Water, 5 cups	

Ingredients to add the Day of Party:

Olive oil, ½ cup	Scallions, chopped, 4 (only green part)
Lemons, 2 (6 tablespoons juice)	
Salt, 2 teaspoons	Parsley, minced, 4 tablespoons
Pepper, ½ teaspoon	Fresh dill, minced, 4 tablespoons
Garlic, crushed, 2 cloves	

Soak beans in water overnight or boil 2 minutes and let soak one hour. Add salt and onion, studded with cloves. Bring to a boil, cover and simmer for 1½ to 2 hours until tender. Drain well and cool.* Pack in freezer container or bag and freeze.

Serving day: Thaw at room temperature for 2 hours. Mix with remaining ingredients and marinate for 3 hours in refrigerator. (Can be done the day before party.) Serve as an appetizer or in a green salad.

To serve without freezing, marinate as directed.

MEAT BALLS ON A TOOTHPICK
(about 160)

Ground beef, 3 pounds

Italian-flavored breadcrumbs,
  ½ cup

Walnuts, finely chopped, ½ cup

Onion, finely chopped, 2

Garlic, crushed, 2 cloves

Grated Parmesan cheese,
  2 tablespoons

Dried basil, 1 teaspoon

Salt, 2 teaspoons

Pepper, ⅛ teaspoon

Paprika, ¼ teaspoon

Eggs, 2, lightly beaten

Sour cream, 4 rounded
  tablespoons

Butter, ½ cup

Garlic, crushed, 2 cloves

Red wine, ½ cup

1. Combine all ingredients except last three and mix thoroughly. Form into small balls about 1″ to 1½″ in diameter.

2. Heat butter and cook garlic for 1 minute. Brown balls on all sides.* Remove balls to freezer container.

3. Add wine to skillet. Heat and scrape up all browned bits. Pour over balls in container. Cool. Cover and freeze.

Serving day: Heat in double-boiler for about 30 to 45 minutes until hot. Add another ½ cup red wine if more liquid is needed. Serve from a chafing dish, with toothpicks available.

To serve without freezing, add wine and simmer for 20 minutes.

MEAT BALLS IN BARBECUE SAUCE
(about 75 balls)

MEAT BALLS

Ground beef, 2 pounds

Onion, finely chopped, 1 large

Cornflake crumbs, 2 tablespoons

Tomato juice, 1½ cups

Salt, 2 teaspoons

Pepper, ½ teaspoon

Paprika, ½ teaspoon

Butter, ½ cup

Garlic, crushed, 2 cloves

SAUCE

Onion, chopped, 1	Worcestershire sauce,
Flour, 1 tablespoon	1 tablespoon
Beef broth, 1½ cups	Tabasco, 2 dashes
Red wine, ½ cup	Brown sugar, 1 tablespoon
Tomato paste, 1 tablespoon	Salt, 1 teaspoon
Chili sauce, 4 tablespoons	Black pepper, ⅛ teaspoon
Lemon juice, 2 tablespoons	Cayenne pepper, ⅛ teaspoon

MEAT BALLS

1. Combine beef, onion, crumbs, tomato juice and seasoning. Gently shape into 1" balls.

2. Sauté garlic in butter for 1 minute. Add balls and brown on all sides. Remove and drain on absorbent paper.

SAUCE

3. In same skillet, sauté onion until golden (about 4 minutes). Remove from fire and blend in flour. Add other ingredients and simmer over low heat for 20 minutes. Stir in meat balls.* Cool. Pack in containers and freeze.

Serving day: Heat, frozen or thawed, in covered double boiler until hot. Serve from chafing dish or serving casserole placed over a heating device.

To serve without freezing, simmer for 15 minutes.

OVEN-BARBECUED PORK SLICES
(60 slices)

Boned loin of pork, in one piece, 3 pounds	Onion, chopped, 1
Soy sauce, ½ cup	Salt, 1 teaspoon
Cider vinegar, 4 tablespoons	Pepper, ½ teaspoon
Oil, 2 tablespoons	Brown sugar, 1 tablespoon
Garlic, crushed, 6 cloves	Curry powder, 1 teaspoon
	Orégano, 1 teaspoon

1. Split meat lengthwise to halve thickness. Combine other ingredients in a large shallow bowl and add meat. Marinate, covered, for 4 hours, turning occasionally.

split meat lengthwise

2. Drain meat and place it in a shallow roasting pan. Roast at 375° F. for 1½ hours, basting occasionally with the marinade.* Remove from pan. Cool. Wrap in foil. Freeze.

Serving day: Reheat, wrapped in foil at 350° F. for 1 hour, until hot. Slice on the diagonal into thin slices. Serve with toothpicks and Chinese mustard (dry mustard mixed with water and a pinch of turmeric).

Ready to slice without freezing.

SHELLFISH CROQUETTES
(about 60 small balls)

Butter, ¼ cup
Flour, ¼ cup
Cream, ½ cup
Milk, ½ cup
Crabmeat or lobster, cooked and chopped, 2 cups
Lemon juice, 2 teaspoons
Onion juice, ½ teaspoon
Parsley, minced, 2 teaspoons
Cumin seed, ¼ teaspoon
Cayenne, ¼ teaspoon
Curry, ¼ teaspoon
Salt, 1 teaspoon
Black pepper, ⅛ teaspoon
Bread crumbs, 1 cup
Eggs, 2

1. Melt butter. Blend in flour. Add cream and milk, stir over low heat until thick and smooth. Mix shellfish, lemon juice, onion juice, parsley and seasoning into cream sauce. Chill for 1 hour or more.

2. Shape into walnut-sized balls. Roll in ½ cup of crumbs. Return to refrigerator for 1 hour or more.

3. Beat eggs slightly. Dip balls into egg and then into the remaining crumbs. Fry in deep fat until brown.* Remove and cool. Freeze on flat surface. When firm, pack and freeze.

Serving day: Heat on a cooky sheet at 400° F. 15 or 20 minutes.

Ready to serve without freezing.

FRIED SHRIMP BALLS
(about 40)

Raw shrimp, peeled and
   deveined, finely chopped,
   1 pound
Raw bacon, finely chopped,
   ½ slice
Canned water chestnuts, finely
   chopped, 5
Scallions, white part only, finely
   chopped, 3 tablespoons

Egg, slightly beaten, 1
Sherry, 1 tablespoon
Baking powder, 1 teaspoon
Cornstarch, 1 tablespoon
Salt, ½ teaspoon
Pepper, ⅛ teaspoon
Sugar, ½ teaspoon
Ground ginger, ¼ teaspoon
Oil for frying, 2 cups

1. Chop together shrimp, bacon, water chestnuts and scallions.
Mix other ingredients together, except oil, and combine with
chopped mixture. Using 2 teaspoons, shape mixture into small
balls the size of large marbles.

2. Heat oil to boiling. Drop in balls a few at a time. Fry till
golden (not brown), and drain on paper towel.* Cool. Freeze on
flat surface. When firm, pack in container and return to freezer.

Serving day: Heat, uncovered, at 375° F. for 15 to 20 minutes.
Serve with following:

SAUCE

Soy sauce, 1 teaspoon
Prepared mustard, 1 teaspoon
Worcestershire sauce, 1 teaspoon
Tobasco sauce, dash
Garlic, crushed, 2 cloves

Catsup, ¼ cup
Beef broth, ½ cup
Cornstarch, 1 tablespoon blended
   with 1 tablespoon water

Combine all ingredients except cornstarch and bring to a boil.
Add cornstarch and blend in. Cool. (Can be made the day before but not frozen.)

       Ready to serve without freezing.

DEVILLED CRAB

(15 scallop shells or 6 individual ramekins—1 quart)

Crab meat, cooked, 3 cups
 (3 6½-oz. cans)
Butter, ¼ pound
Onion, chopped, 1
Flour, 3 tablespoons
Dry mustard, 1 teaspoon
Paprika, ½ teaspoon
Salt, ¾ teaspoon
Cayenne pepper, ⅛ teaspoon
Worcestershire sauce, ½ teaspoon

Milk, ½ cup
Cream, ½ cup
Sherry, ¼ cup
Chives, minced, 2 tablespoons
Mushrooms, sliced, ½ cup
 (3-oz. can)
Bread crumbs, ⅓ cup
Parmesan cheese, grated, ½ cup
Paprika, 2 teaspoons

1. Remove cartilage from crabmeat and flake. Heat 3 tablespoons butter. Add onion and cook over low heat until golden. Blend in flour and seasonings. Add milk. Cook over low heat, stirring frequently until thickened. Stir in cream, sherry, chives, mushrooms, and crabmeat.

2. Fill shells. Melt remaining butter and mix with crumbs. Sprinkle shells with crumbs, grated cheese, and paprika.* Freeze. When frozen, wrap each shell in foil.

Serving day: Remove foil and bake at 375° F. for 25 minutes.

To serve without freezing, bake in 375° F. oven for 15 to 20 minutes.

LOBSTER CHUNKS WITH SOUR CREAM DIP

(about 24 chunks)

8-ounce lobster tails, 2
Water, 4 quarts
Salt, 2 tablespoons

Pepper, ¼ teaspoon
Celery seed, 1 teaspoon
Vinegar, 2 tablespoons

Place water, seasoning, and vinegar in a large kettle and bring to a boil. Add lobster tails and boil for 12 minutes. Remove and place in cold water. Using scissors, split underside and pull away membrane. Insert fingers under lobster and remove from shell. Cut into bite-sized chunks.* Cool, pack and freeze.

split
underside

insert fingers under lobster
meat and remove from shell

Night before serving: Remove lobster to refrigerator and prepare dip.

DIP

Chive cream cheese,
  3-oz. package
Sour cream, ½ cup
Salt, ½ teaspoon

Sugar, ½ teaspoon
Horseradish, 2 tablespoons
Minced chives, 1 tablespoon

Soften cheese and blend with other ingredients.
*Chill to serve without freezing.

*place on
broiler pan
rounded side up*

BROILED HAM-STUFFED MUSHROOMS

Mushrooms, medium, 100
  (about 3 pounds)
Butter, 5 tablespoons
Onion, finely chopped, 3
Boiled ham, minced, 1¼ cups
  (about ½ pound)
Dry mustard, ¼ teaspoon

Fresh parsley, minced,
  2 tablespoons
Sour cream, ¼ cup
Chopped almonds, 1 cup
Salt, ¼ teaspoon
Pepper, pinch

1. Wash mushrooms. Remove stems and chop them fine. Melt 3 tablespoons of butter in skillet and sauté onions and chopped stems. Add rest of ingredients, except caps.

2. Brush caps all over with 2 tablespoons melted butter. Place on broiling pan, rounded side up, and broil for 1 minute. Remove and fill cups with stuffing.*

3. Place on flat surface and freeze until firm. Pack in plastic bag or containers and return to freezer.

Serving day: Brush with melted butter and broil 4 minutes under medium flame.

*To serve without freezing, broil as directed.

HOT MUSHROOM HORS D'OEUVRE

Butter, ½ pound	Salt, 2¼ teaspoons
Mushrooms, thinly sliced, 3 pounds	Pepper, ¼ teaspoon
	Paprika, 1½ teaspoons
Onions, sliced, 10 medium	Sour cream, 1 cup

Melt butter in large pan. Add mushrooms, onions, and seasoning and cook, uncovered, for 2½ hours, stirring occasionally.* Cool. Pack in container. Freeze.

Serving day: Heat in double boiler or over low heat until hot. Stir in sour cream and cook without boiling, uncovered, over low direct heat for another 30 minutes until creamy and thick. Serve on plates with or without toast, or in Puff Paste Croustades (see index) or in patty shells.

Note: This is a good waiting dish. Extra warming does not hurt as long as it never boils.

To serve without freezing, stir in sour cream and heat another 30 minutes.

MARINATED PEPPERS

Green peppers, 10	Ice water, 1 bowl

Ingredients to Add the Day of Party:

Olive oil, ¼ cup	Salt, ¼ teaspoon
Lemon juice, 2 tablespoons	Pepper, pinch
Wine vinegar, 1 tablespoon	Rolled anchovy fillets, 1 can
Garlic, crushed, 2 cloves	

1. Wash and dry peppers. Place them under the direct flame of the broiler or over the flame of a gas burner. Turn until they are charred all over.

2. Remove to bowl of ice water and rub and peel off skin. Cut in half, cut off stems and wash out seeds. Drain on absorbent paper. Cut peppers into eighths, lengthwise.* Pack in container. Freeze.

Day before or *Serving day:* Thaw peppers at room temperature for 2 hours. Combine with oil, lemon juice, vinegar, garlic, salt and pepper. Marinate for 4 or more hours. Arrange on a serving platter, decorated with anchovies.

To serve without freezing, marinate as directed.

sear peppers
over gas flame

bread

3

ON BREAD MAKING

Making bread is not difficult nor does it require a lot of your active time. The yeast-rising process involves waiting, but you can be doing other things while listening for the timer to warn you that the next bread-making operation should be started.

On a Warm Place for Rising: The temperature should be 80° to 85° F. Examples are: on an asbestos mat, over the pilot light of a gas range; on the top shelf of a closed, unheated oven with a pan of boiling water on the oven floor; or in the dishwasher, sitting on a rack placed over a pan of hot water. Always cover and keep away from drafts.

lift dough and fold down towards you

On Kneading: Knead by lifting the dough with fingers spread, folding it down on itself and toward you, and then lightly pressing down and away with the heel of the hand. Turn the ball a quarter circle and repeat entire motion. Repeat this rhythmically for 8 to 10 minutes until dough which was sticky becomes smooth and elastic and does not stick to the board.

CHEESE BREAD
(2 loaves or 1 long twist)

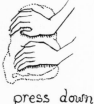

press down and away

Ginger, ⅛ teaspoon
Warm water, ¾ cup
Dry yeast, 1 package
Sugar, 2 tablespoons
Milk, scalded and cooled to
  lukewarm, 1 cup
Flour, 4¾ cups
Eggs, 2
Soft butter, 2 tablespoons

Salt, 1½ teaspoons
Paprika, ½ teaspoon
Sharp Cheddar cheese, coarsely
  grated, 1¼ cups (about
  5 ounces)
Toasted sesame seeds,
  6 tablespoons
Egg yolk, 1

1. Stir together ginger and ¼ cup warm water. Sprinkle in yeast and stir until dissolved. Let stand in a warm place until thickened (about 3 or 4 minutes). Stir together sugar, ½ cup water, milk and 1½ cups flour. Using a wooden spoon, vigorously beat in the yeast mixture until smooth.

2. Beat in eggs, 1 at a time. Stir in butter, salt, paprika, grated cheese, and sesame seeds. Add 2½ cups flour gradually and stir until flour leaves the sides of the bowl.

3. Spread ¾ cup flour on board. Turn out dough and knead well for 6 to 8 minutes, until dough is elastic and no longer sticky. (Sprinkle a little extra flour on board if necessary.)

4. Put dough in a lightly greased bowl. Grease top, cover with cloth and let rise in warm place about 45 minutes or until doubled.

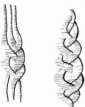

braid dough
starting from middle

5. Turn out on board and knead lightly for 1 minute. Divide dough in half and shape into loaves, fit into 2 greased 9" loaf pans. Or divide dough into 3 equal parts. Roll each part into a long strip, tapered at the ends. Place the 3 strips on a greased jelly-roll pan, and braid them together, starting from the middle. Brush tops with egg yolk beaten with water, sprinkle with remaining sesame seeds. Cover and let rise in warm place about 40 minutes.

6. Bake at 350° F. for 15 minutes. Reduce heat to 325° F. for 30 minutes. (Top should be brown and sides shrunk away from sides of loaf pans.) Turn out of pans and cool on rack.* When cool, wrap and freeze.

Serving day: Thaw, wrapped, at room temperature, for about 1 hour. Slice. Wrap in foil or in a brown paper bag and heat for 5 or 10 minutes at 350° F. Serve slightly warm.

Ready to slice without freezing.

HERB SPIRAL BREAD

(2 loaves)

SPONGE

Ginger, ⅛ teaspoon
Sugar, 2½ tablespoons
Warm water, ¼ cup
Dry yeast, 1 package

Flour, sifted, 2 cups
Milk, scalded and cooled to
    lukewarm, 1¼ cups

FILLING

Butter, 2 tablespoons
Garlic, crushed, 2 cloves
Fresh dill, minced, 1 cup
Parsley, minced, 2 cups
Scallions, minced, 1 cup
    (green part only)

Eggs, lightly beaten, 2
Salt, ¾ teaspoon
Pepper, ⅛ teaspoon
Tabasco sauce, dash

DOUGH

Sponge (see beginning of recipe)
Warm water, 1½ cups
Salt, 2½ teaspoons

Melted butter, 4 tablespoons
Flour, sifted, 5½ cups

SPONGE

1. Stir together ginger, ½ teaspoon sugar and lukewarm water. Sprinkle on yeast and stir until dissolved. Let stand in a warm place until thickened and bubbly (about 3 or 4 minutes).

2. In a large bowl, stir together remaining sugar, flour and milk. Using a wooden spoon, vigorously beat in the yeast mixture until smooth. Cover bowl and let stand in a warm place 45 minutes to 1 hour until well risen and bubbly.

FILLING

3. Melt butter and cook garlic, dill, parsley and scallions over medium heat, stirring occasionally until wilted, but not brown. Cool. Beat eggs lightly and reserve 2 tablespoons for brushing on dough. Stir remaining egg and seasoning into cooled herbs. Refrigerate until needed.

DOUGH

4. Add warm water, salt and butter to sponge. Beat well with a wooden spoon. Gradually add 4½ cups flour, stirring it down from the sides of the bowl until well blended and the dough clears the bowl.

5. Spread remaining cup of flour on pastry board. Turn out dough and knead well for 10 minutes, until smooth and elastic. Return to bowl and dust with flour. Cover with a damp cloth and let rise in a warm place for about 30 minutes.

6. Turn out on a board and knead thoroughly for 5 minutes, using extra flour if necessary to keep dough from sticking. Divide dough in half and shape each half into a ball. Cover and let rest 10 minutes. Roll out each ball with a rolling pin into a rectangle about 9″ wide and ¼″ thick.

roll like a jelly-roll

7. Brush with 2 tablespoons of beaten egg and then spread on filling to about 1″ from the edges. Roll up like a jelly roll, starting from the 9″ edge, and pinch edges to seal. Place in greased loaf pans (about 9″ x 5″ x 3″) with seam side down. Brush tops with melted butter. Cover with a cloth and let rise in warm place for 1 hour, until doubled.

8. Bake at 350° F. for 20 minutes. Reduce heat to 325° F. and bake for 25 minutes. Remove from pans to wire rack and cool.* Wrap in foil or plastic bag and freeze.

Serving day: Thaw bread, wrapped, at room temperature for 1 hour. Slice. Wrap in foil or a brown paper bag. Before serving, heat at 350° F. for 10 to 15 minutes.

Ready to slice without freezing.

TOMATO JUICE BREAD

(2 loaves)

Ginger, ¼ teaspoon
Sugar, ¼ cup plus 1 teaspoon
Warm water, ½ cup
Dry yeast, 2 packages
Tomato juice, lukewarm,
    1½ cups

Flour, 5¾ cups
Melted butter, ¼ cup
Salt, 2 teaspoons
Orégano, 1 teaspoon
Dill seed, 2 tablespoons

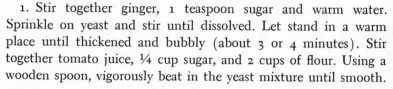

stir until dough clears the sides of bowl

1. Stir together ginger, 1 teaspoon sugar and warm water. Sprinkle on yeast and stir until dissolved. Let stand in a warm place until thickened and bubbly (about 3 or 4 minutes). Stir together tomato juice, ¼ cup sugar, and 2 cups of flour. Using a wooden spoon, vigorously beat in the yeast mixture until smooth.

2. Stir in melted butter and seasoning. Gradually add 3¼ cups flour, stirring it down from the sides of the bowl until well blended and the dough clears sides of the bowl.

3. Spread remaining ½ cup flour on pastry board. Turn out dough and knead well for 10 minutes, until smooth and elastic. Put dough in a lightly greased bowl. Grease top, cover with cloth and let rise in warm place about 45 minutes or until doubled.

after kneading, cover dough. let rise until........doubled

4. Turn out on board and knead lightly for 1 minute. Divide dough in half and shape into loaves. Fit into 2 greased 9″ loaf pans. Brush tops with butter. Cover and let rise in warm place about 45 minutes, until doubled.

5. Bake in 350° F. oven for 50 minutes. Remove from pans to wire rack and cool.* Wrap in foil or plastic bags. Freeze.

Serving day: Thaw wrapped, at room temperature for about 1 hour. Slice. Wrap slices in foil or in a brown paper bag and heat for 5 or 10 minutes in a 350° F. oven. Serve slightly warm.

*Ready to serve without freezing.

ONION ROLLS
(about 28)

Dehydrated onion flakes,
  3 tablespoons
Boiling water, 1 cup
Soft butter, 4 tablespoons
Salt, 1½ teaspoons
Sugar, 2 tablespoons

Ginger, ⅛ teaspoon
Warm water, ¼ cup
Dry yeast, 1 package
Egg, 1
Dried dill weed, 2 tablespoons
Flour, 3 cups

1. Combine onion flakes and boiling water. Cover and let stand for 15 minutes. Place butter, salt and sugar in a bowl. Drain onion flakes, reserving them, and reheat liquid. Pour hot liquid over ingredients in bowl and stir until they are dissolved.

2. Combine ginger, warm water and yeast. Let stand in a warm place for 3 or 4 minutes. When butter mixture has cooled to lukewarm, beat in yeast. Beat in egg with a wire whisk. Stir in drained onions and dill. Gradually add flour and beat in with a wooden spoon until well blended and a soft dough is formed.

3. Turn out dough into a large greased bowl. Turn over to grease top. Cover bowl tightly with foil and refrigerate for 2 to 12 hours, until doubled.

fill tins ⅓ full
and cover

let rise
until doubled

4. Punch down dough. Pinch off pieces and fill greased muffin tins ⅓ full. Cover and let rise in a warm place for 30 minutes until doubled in bulk. Bake at 425° F. for 12 minutes until golden but not brown. Remove immediately from pans and cool on a rack.* Wrap in a plastic bag. Freeze.

Serving day: Thaw, wrapped, at room temperature for 15 to 20 minutes. Heat, wrapped in foil or paper bag, at 350° F. for 5 minutes.

Ready to serve without freezing.

TOASTED ALMOND MUFFINS
(about 32)

Soft butter, 6 tablespoons
Sugar, 2 tablespoons
Eggs, 4
Sour cream, 1 cup
Ground ginger, ¼ teaspoon
Warm water, 2 tablespoons
Dry yeast, 1 package

Flour, sifted, 3¼ cups
Salt, 2 teaspoons
Soda, 1 teaspoon
Toasted slivered almonds, 1 cup
Toasted chopped almonds,
   ¼ cup

1. Cream together butter and sugar with a wooden spoon. Beat eggs and beat into butter. Add sour cream.

2. Combine ginger, warm water and yeast and let stand, covered, in a warm place for 3 or 4 minutes. Beat into egg mixture. Sift together flour, salt and soda and gradually beat into the liquid mixture. Stir in slivered almonds.

shape into balls

3. Wet hands and shape dough into balls, filling greased muffin tins about half full. Sprinkle tops with a few chopped almonds. Cover and let rolls rise in a warm place until doubled (about 1 hour).

4. Bake on an upper shelf at 375° F. for 15 minutes.* Cool. Pack into container or bag. Freeze.

Serving day: Wrap muffins in foil and heat at 350° F. until warm.

Ready to slice without freezing.

ROQUEFORT CHEESE BISCUITS
(about 16 2½" biscuits)

Flour, sifted, 2 cups
Baking powder, 3 teaspoons
Sugar, 1 tablespoon
Salt, ½ teaspoon
Butter or shortening,
   6 tablespoons

Roquefort cheese, crumbled,
   3 tablespoons
Milk, ¾ cup
Egg yolk, 1

1. Sift together flour, baking powder, sugar and salt. Cut in butter with a pastry blender until it reaches texture of coarse cornmeal. Stir in cheese. Make a well in the center of ingredients. Pour in milk and stir until all flour disappears and dough leaves the sides of the bowl and forms a soft dough. (This should take about 30 seconds.)

2. Turn out dough onto a lightly floured board. Knead gently for 10 fold-overs. Roll out with a floured rolling pin to ½″ thickness. Cut into rounds with a floured biscuit cutter, 2″ or 2½″ in diameter. Brush the tops with an egg yolk, mixed with 1 tablespoon water.

3. Place them on an ungreased cooky sheet. Bake at 425° F. for 15 minutes until golden brown. Immediately remove from pans and cool.* Wrap in plastic bag. Freeze.

Serving day: Wrap in foil or paper bag and heat at 300° F. for 10 to 15 minutes.

Ready to serve without freezing.

QUICK ONION BREAD

lay onion
slices on top

White bread, unsliced, 1 loaf   Egg, 1
Butter, ¼ pound   Onion, thinly sliced, 1

Remove crusts from bread and place on baking dish. Melt butter and brush liberally on sides of loaf. Beat egg and brush on top of loaf. Lay slices of onion on top and brush on remaining butter. Put under broiler and toast top.* Wrap in foil. Freeze.

Serving day: Heat, wrapped, at 350° F. for 15 minutes before serving. Cut in thick slices.

Ready to serve without freezing.

QUICK HERB BREAD
(8 servings)

Butter, ¼ pound   Dried basil, ½ teaspoon
Parsley, minced, 1 tablespoon   White bread, unsliced, 1 loaf
Chives, minced, 1 tablespoon

1. Cream butter and blend with herbs. Remove crusts from bread and cut into thick slices.

2. Place bread on large piece of foil. Spread butter on both sides of each slice and press back into loaf form. Cut through the middle the long way. Wrap foil around loaf.* Freeze.

Serving day: Heat, wrapped, at 400° F. for 20 minutes.

> *To serve without freezing, heat, wrapped, at 400° F. for 10 minutes.*

GARLIC BREAD
(6 to 8 servings)

Butter, ¼ pound

Garlic, crushed, 4 cloves
French bread, 1 loaf

1. Melt butter and cook with garlic over low heat, for one minute.

2. Put bread on sheet of aluminum foil. Cut in 1″ diagonal slices, almost to the bottom. Spread slices apart. Brush butter generously between the slices. Press back into loaf and brush the sides and top.* Wrap foil tightly around bread. Freeze.

Serving day: Open foil. Bake at 350° F. for 15 minutes.

> *To serve without freezing, wrap foil around bread, leaving top open. Bake in 350° F. oven for 10 minutes.*

EXTRA NOTES ON BREAD

Yeast dough should not be frozen unbaked, but rolls can be partially prepared by baking at 275° F. for about 20 minutes. To serve, thaw at room temperature for 15 minutes and bake at 450° F. for 5 to 10 minutes until golden brown, or unthawed at 350° F. for 30 minutes until golden brown.

Fully cooked breads should be wrapped in foil or a paper bag and heated in a 350° F. oven until hot. They will taste fresher than if thawed at room temperature. If you do thaw instead of heat, leave bread wrapped.

brush garlic butter between slices

soup

4

BEEF STOCK
(3 quarts)

eject cubes....
pack in bag

Veal or beef bones
Shin of beef, plate, chuck,
  or flanken, 4 or 4½ pounds
Water, 4 quarts
Onion, quartered, 2
Parsley root, sliced, 2
Celery, sliced, 3 stalks with leaves
Carrots, sliced, 4

Parsley, 4 or 5 sprigs
Leeks, chopped, 1 or 2
Salt, 2 tablespoons
Peppercorns, 8 or 10
Bay leaves, 2
Thyme, ¼ teaspoon
Dill, powdered or seed,
  ½ teaspoon

1. Sear meat quickly in a large kettle without additional shortening. Add bones and water. Bring to a boil and remove scum. Add remaining ingredients. Cover and simmer for 4 to 5 hours.

2. Remove meat and strain stock. Chill until fat congeals. Remove fat.* Pack in small containers and freeze, or cook down to a more concentrated stock and freeze in ice-cube trays. When frozen, eject cubes and pack in freezer bag.

Serving day: The stock can be combined with vegetables or barley and served as soup or used in sauces.

    Reheat to serve without freezing.

CHICKEN STOCK
(3½ quarts, 12 to 14 servings)

Fowl, split, 5 to 6 pounds
Cold water, 4 quarts
Carrots, sliced, 2
Onion, quartered, 2
Celery, including leaves, 3 stalks
Parsnip, sliced, 2

Leeks, sliced, 2
Parsley, 6 sprigs
Fresh dill, 6 sprigs
Tomato sauce, ½ small can
Salt, 1 tablespoon
Pepper, ¾ teaspoon

1. Place fowl in large kettle with cold water. Cover and bring to a boil. Remove scum. Add vegetables, tomato sauce, and seasonings. Cover and simmer for 3 hours.

2. Remove chicken. Strain soup, pressing vegetables through a colander. Chill soup. Remove congealed fat.* Pour into containers and freeze.

Serving day: Heat in covered double boiler or over low heat. Serve with noodles, rice, etc.

Note: Package in ½-pint containers for easy use in recipes where stock is needed. When frozen, remove from container and wrap in foil. Or cook down to a more concentrated stock and freeze in ice-cube trays. When frozen, eject cubes and pack in freezer bags.

remove from container....wrap in foil

*Reheat to serve without freezing.

BLACK BEAN SOUP
(½ gallon)

Black beans, 2 cups	Thyme, ¼ teaspoon
Cold water, 2 quarts	Cayenne pepper, ⅛ teaspoon
Salt pork, diced, ¼ pound	Orégano, ¼ teaspoon
Garlic, crushed, 4 cloves	Curry powder, ¼ teaspoon
Onion, finely chopped, 2	(optional)
Green pepper, finely chopped, 2	Wine vinegar, 3 tablespoons
Salt, 2 teaspoons	Sherry, ½ cup
Bay leaves, 2	Lemon slices

1. Soak beans in 2 quarts of water overnight or boil 2 minutes and let soak, covered, for 1 hour.

2. Add to beans, salt pork, garlic, onion, green pepper, seasonings and wine vinegar. Cover and simmer for 2½ hours. Purée in blender or through sieve.* Cool. Pack in container. Freeze.

Serving day: Reheat in double boiler or over very low heat. Before serving, stir in sherry and heat through. Serve topped with lemon slices.

*To serve without freezing, reheat and stir in sherry.

RUSSIAN CABBAGE SOUP

(1½ gallons)

Chuck roast, 4 pounds
Lemons, 2
Cabbage, shredded, 3 quarts
  (2½ pounds)
Carrots, sliced, 2
Onion, sliced, 2 large
Whole tomatoes, 4 cups
  (2 pound, 3-ounce can)

Julienne beets, 2 cups
  (1 pound can)
Borscht, 1 quart jar
Water, 2½ quarts
Salt, 2 tablespoons
Pepper, ½ teaspoon
Brown sugar, 4 tablespoons
Dill seeds, 3 teaspoons
Caraway seeds, 3 teaspoons

1. Cut surplus fat from meat and sear in heavy skillet. Transfer to large soup kettle.

2. Extract juice from lemons and add to meat with whole rind. Add cabbage, carrots, onions, tomatoes, beets, borscht, water, and seasonings. Cover and simmer for 6 or 7 hours.

3. Remove meat and lemon rind. Chill soup. Remove congealed fat.* Freeze soup and meat separately.

Serving day: Reheat over low fire or in double boiler.

Serve with or without meat, with sour cream, dark bread, cheese, smoked salmon or whitefish, platters of pickled cucumbers and red onions, hard-boiled eggs, etc. Or follow with cold poached salmon with a chopped cucumber and sour cream sauce.

Reheat to serve without freezing.

FRESH GREEN PEA SOUP

(2 quarts)

Fresh peas, 2 pounds
Butter, 2 tablespoons
Leeks, chopped, 2
Fresh spinach, shredded,
  ½ pound
Boston lettuce, shredded, 1 head
Water, 1 cup

Salt, 2 teaspoons
White pepper, ¼ teaspoon
Chicken broth, 3 cups
Mint jelly, 2 tablespoons
Sherry, ¼ cup
Heavy cream, ½ cup

1. Shell peas, reserving 10 pods. Melt butter in a large saucepan. Sauté leeks until wilted. Add spinach, lettuce, water, salt, pepper, peas and reserved pods. Cover and simmer for about 40 minutes until peas are very soft.

2. Remove pea pods and purée mixture in the blender. Heat broth and stir in pea purée and mint jelly until well blended.* Cool. Pack in containers. Freeze.

3. Whip the cream and place spoonfuls in cone-shaped mounds on flat surface. Freeze until firm and pack in container.

Serving day: Reheat over low heat. Before serving, stir in sherry and heat through. Defrost whipped cream at room temperature for 15 minutes. Serve soup, topped with whipped cream mounds.

*To serve without freezing, stir in sherry and heat. Serve topped with whipped cream.

whipped cream in mounds on flat surface

MUSHROOM SOUP
(2½ quarts)

Dried mushrooms, ½ ounce	Parsley, minced, ½ cup
Warm water, ½ cup	Beef broth, 2 quarts
Butter, 4 tablespoons	Salt, 1 tablespoon (or to taste)
Fresh mushrooms, coarsely	Sherry, ½ cup
chopped, 1 pound	Egg yolk, 1
Paprika, 2 teaspoons	Sour cream, ½ cup
Flour, 1½ tablespoons	

1. Rinse dried mushrooms, cut up, and soak in ½ cup warm water for 45 minutes.

2. Heat butter and sauté fresh mushrooms over low heat for 4 or 5 minutes. Sprinkle with paprika, flour and parsley. Stir in beef broth, dried mushrooms with soaking liquid, salt and sherry. Simmer for 1 hour.* Cool. Pack in container. Freeze.

Serving day: Reheat over low heat. When hot, beat egg yolks lightly with sour cream. Blend in a little hot soup and gradually stir into soup. Serve hot with croutons.

*To serve without freezing, stir in egg yolks and cream as directed.

cut up dried mushrooms and soak

GAZPACHO

(8 to 10 servings)

dip tomatoes
into boiling water,

then, into
ice water

and peel.

Tomatoes, peeled, 8
Cucumber, peeled and
  chopped, 1
Green pepper, chopped, 2
Garlic, crushed, 3 cloves
Red or sweet onion, chopped, 1
White bread, ½ slice
Lime juice, 3 tablespoons
Olive oil, ⅓ cup
Fresh chives, chopped, 1 table-
  spoon (or ½ teaspoon dried)

Fresh basil chopped, 1 tablespoon
  (or ½ teaspoon dried)
Salt, 1½ teaspoons
Black pepper, ¼ teaspoon
Chicken or veal broth, 1 cup
Cream, sweet or sour, ¼ cup
Cucumber, peeled and diced,
  1 cup
Cantaloupe or honeydew melon,
  ½ cup
Seedless grapes, ½ cup

Purée tomatoes in blender or through food mill with chopped cucumber, green pepper, garlic, onion, bread with crusts removed, lime juice, oil, herbs and seasoning. Add chicken broth and blend well.* Pour into container. Freeze.

Serving day: Thaw at room temperature for several hours or overnight in refrigerator. Add cream and blend in blender or with beater until smooth. Spoon diced cucumber, melon, and grapes into soup bowls, then ladle in soup. Serve well chilled.

> **To serve without freezing, blend in cream and chill. Serve as directed.*

SPICY TOMATO SOUP

(1 gallon and 1 pint)

celery knob
(or celeriac)

Beef broth, 3 quarts (see index)
Canned whole tomatoes, 4
  1-pound cans (about 8 cups)
Celery knob, peeled and sliced,
  1½ to 2 pounds
Garlic, crushed, 2 cloves
Fresh parsley, minced, ¼ cup

Fresh dill, minced, ¼ cup
Thyme, 1½ teaspoons
Bay leaf, 1
Celery seed, 1 teaspoon
Sugar, 2 teaspoons
Crushed red pepper, ½ teaspoon
Salt, 2 teaspoons

1. Put stock in soup kettle. Crush tomatoes and, with their liquid, add to kettle. Add other ingredients and bring to a boil. Cover and simmer for 45 minutes to an hour.

2. Strain liquid through a colander. Discard bay leaf and purée vegetables in a food mill or blender. Stir the purée into the liquid until blended.* Cool. Pour into freezing containers and freeze.

Serving day: Reheat over low heat. Serve with avocado slices or garlic croutons and a sprinkling of chopped fresh dill.

> *To serve without freezing, reheat and garnish as directed.*

SPINACH SOUP
(about 3 quarts)

Frozen leaf spinach, 4 10-ounce packages or 4 pounds fresh	Paprika, ½ teaspoon
Butter, 4 tablespoons	Whole nutmeg, grated, ½ teaspoon
Scallions, chopped, 1 cup	Sherry, 1 cup
Salt, 2½ teaspoons	Sour cream
Fresh dill, minced, ½ cup	Almonds, toasted and chopped
Chicken broth, 8 cups	Grated cheese

1. Defrost frozen spinach for 3 hours or wash fresh spinach.

2. Heat butter in large saucepan and sauté scallions until golden. Add spinach and sauté, stirring occasionally, until wilted. Add salt, cover and cook until tender. Stir in dill and cook 1 minute. Put mixture with the liquid in blender and purée.

3. Return purée to pan and stir in chicken broth, paprika and nutmeg until well mixed.* Cool. Pack in container. Freeze.

Serving day: Reheat over low heat until boiling. Stir in sherry and heat through. Serve in hot soup bowls, garnished with sour cream, chopped almonds, grated cheese, and a little freshly grated nutmeg.

> *To serve without freezing, stir in sherry and heat through. Garnish as directed.*

VICHYSSOISE
(about 10 cups)

Butter, 3 tablespoons
Leeks, sliced, 3 cups
Onion, chopped, 1
Potatoes, peeled and sliced,
   5 cups
Chicken broth, 3 cups
Salt, 2 teaspoons
White pepper, ½ teaspoon

Curry, ½ teaspoon
Dry mustard, ¼ teaspoon
Milk, 2 cups
Watercress leaves, 1 cup
Light cream, 1 cup
Heavy cream, 1 cup
Chopped chives

slice potatoes
and leeks

1. Heat butter in a large kettle and sauté leeks and onion until soft but not browned (4 or 5 minutes). Add potatoes, chicken broth and salt and simmer, covered, for 30 minutes. Purée in blender.

2. Return to heat. Add milk and seasoning and bring to a boil. Purée watercress in blender with some soup. Add to soup and cook for 2 or 3 minutes. Cool.* Pack in 2 quart containers. Freeze.

Night before serving: Thaw overnight in refrigerator, or at room temperature for 6 hours. Break up icy lumps with a knife or fork and reblend in the blender, adding a little of the light cream if necessary. Stir in remaining cream. Refrigerate. Serve in cups with a sprinkling of chopped chives.

> **To serve without freezing, stir in cream and chill in refrigerator.*

MUSSEL SOUP
(5 cups)

Mussels, 3 pounds
Water, 3 cups
Salt, 1½ teaspoons
Onion, chopped, 1
Parsley, 3 sprigs
Dill, 3 sprigs
Carrot, chopped, 1
Green pepper, chopped, ¼ cup

Garlic, crushed, 1 clove
White wine, 1 cup
Bay leaf, 1
Thyme, 1 teaspoon
Cayenne, ⅛ teaspoon
Heavy cream, 1 cup
Egg yolks, 2

cook till shells open

1. Soak mussels in cold water for 15 minutes, then scrub them under running water with a stiff brush and cut off beards. Place them in a pot with the 3 cups water and salt and cook until shells open. Strain cooking liquid through a colander lined with a double thickness of cheesecloth and remove mussels from the shells.

2. Place strained liquid and mussels in a pot with the onion, parsley, dill, carrot, green pepper, garlic, wine and seasoning. Cover and simmer for 1 hour.

3. Strain again. Chop mussels coarsely and return to soup.* Cool. Pack in quart container. Freeze.

Serving day: Reheat soup over low heat until boiling. Stir in cream and heat through. Beat egg yolks lightly. Beat in 1 cup of hot soup and then stir into soup. Heat through until slightly thickened but do not boil. Serve hot with sea toast.

strain through cheesecloth

> *To serve without freezing, reheat soup and stir in cream and egg yolk as directed.*

CRAB MEAT BISQUE
(8 to 10 servings, 3 pints)

Butter, 3 tablespoons
Onion, chopped, 1
Mushrooms, chopped, 1 cup
  (¼ pound)
Crabmeat, fresh or canned,
  2 cups
Tomato, peeled and chopped, 1
Parsley, minced, 2 tablespoons
Chives, minced, 2 tablespoons

Fish stock, clam or chicken
  broth, 2 cups
Salt, 1 tablespoon
Pepper, ⅛ teaspoon
Nutmeg, ⅛ teaspoon
Curry, ¼ teaspoon
Flour, 1 tablespoon
Cream, ½ cup
Sherry, ½ cup
Fresh dill, chopped

1. Heat 2 tablespoons of butter. Sauté onion and mushrooms over low heat for about 5 minutes.

2. Remove cartilage from crabmeat and flake. Stir into onion and mushrooms with tomato, parsley and chives and cook for 3 or 4 minutes. Add 1 cup of stock and seasoning. Purée in blender.

3. Heat remaining tablespoon of butter. Blend in flour until smooth. Gradually stir in fish purée and remaining stock until well blended.* Cool. Pack in container. Freeze.

Serving day: Heat over low heat until very hot. Before serving, stir in cream and sherry and heat through. Serve in cups and garnish with chopped dill.

> **To serve without freezing, reheat and stir in cream and sherry.*

BOUILLABAISSE
(8 to 10 servings)

Fish heads and bones,
 1½ pounds
Water, 2 quarts
Onion, coarsely chopped, 1
Carrot, sliced, 1
Celery, sliced, 2 stalks with leaves
Bay leaf, 1
Salt, 1 teaspoon
Peppercorns, 5
Oil, ½ cup
Garlic, crushed, 2 cloves
Onions, finely chopped, 1 cup
Celery, chopped, 2 stalks
Leeks, chopped, 2
Fresh parsley, minced, ½ cup

Canned whole tomatoes, 2 cups
 (1-lb. can)
Thyme, ½ teaspoon
Bay leaf, 1
Fennel seeds, crushed,
 ½ teaspoon
Saffron, 1 teaspoon
Salt, 1 teaspoon
Cayenne, ⅛ teaspoon
Dry white wine, 1 cup
Frozen lobster tails, 4
Fillet of haddock, red snapper or
 cod, 3 pounds, cut into
 serving pieces
Raw shrimp, peeled and
 deveined, 24
Mussels, 16 (optional)

1. Wash the fish heads and bones, and place in a large kettle with the water, onions, carrot, celery, bay leaf, salt and pepper. Bring to a boil and simmer for 30 minutes. Strain and reserve the stock.

2. Heat oil in a large pot. Cook garlic for ½ minute. Add onions, celery, leeks, and parsley. Cook until wilted. Add tomatoes, seasoning, wine and reserved fish stock. Bring to a boil and simmer for 10 minutes.

3. Add lobster. Cook for 5 minutes. Add fish and cook for 5 minutes. Add shrimp and cook for 5 more minutes.

4. Remove soup from fire. Lift out lobster and place in cold water. Split shells with scissors and remove lobster meat. Cut it into large chunks. Discard shells and put lobster back into soup.* Cool soup. Pack in large container, separating half way with a sheet of foil. Freeze.

Serving day: Heat over low fire until thoroughly hot. If too thick add a cup of canned clam juice or broth. Scrub mussels very well and remove beards. Place in a large kettle of boiling water seasoned with pepper and thyme. Cover and cook until shells open.

Ladle the fish and mussels in the shell into a hot serving platter. Pour the soup into a hot tureen. Place a large slice of garlic-rubbed toasted French bread in each hot soup plate and serve the fish and soup ladled over it.

> *To serve without freezing, reheat, cook mussels, and serve as directed.*

SOUPE DE POISSONS MEDITERRANEE

(6 quarts)

Whole red snapper, 3½ pounds
Whole sea bass, 3½ pounds
Water, 3 quarts
Celery, sliced, 3 stalks with tops
Onion, sliced, 1
Carrot, sliced, 1
Bay leaves, 2
Salt, 1½ teaspoons
Peppercorns, 10

Oil, ¾ cup
Garlic, crushed, 2
Leeks, chopped, 6

Celery, chopped, 6 stalks
Fennel, chopped, 2 bulbs, or
    ½ teaspoon fennel seed
Onion, chopped, 2
Parsley, 6 sprigs
Canned whole tomatoes, 4 cups
    (2-lb., 3-oz. can)
Thyme, 1½ teaspoons
Saffron, ½ teaspoon
Pepper, ¼ teaspoon
Salt, 3 teaspoons
Dry white wine, 1 cup
Clams in shell, 1 dozen

fennel
(or finocchio)

1. Have the fish cleaned, skinned and the head and bones removed. Wash the head and bones and put them into a large kettle with the water, celery, onion, carrot, bay leaves, salt, and peppercorns. Bring to a boil and simmer for 30 minutes. Strain and reserve the stock.

2. Heat oil in large pot. Cook garlic for ½ minute. Add leeks, celery, fennel, onion, and parsley. Cook until wilted. Add tomatoes, seasoning, wine, 2 quarts of the reserved fish stock, and the fish fillets. Simmer for 45 minutes. Wash clams thoroughly and add to soup. Simmer for 15 minutes. Remove clams and reserve.

3. Force soup and fish through food mill or purée in blender. Remove clams from shell and chop coarsely and add to soup.* Cool. Pack in freezer containers. Freeze.

Serving day: Heat in double boiler or over low heat until thoroughly hot. Serve with fried garlic croutons or vermicelli.

Note: Whitefish, flounder, or haddock can be used if red snapper or bass is unavailable.

> **To serve without freezing, reheat and serve as directed.*

meat

STEAK AND KIDNEY PIE
(8 servings)

Beef round, 4 pounds
Veal kidneys, 3
Flour, ¼ cup
Salt, 1 teaspoon
Pepper, ¼ teaspoon
Powdered mace, ¼ teaspoon
Dry mustard, 1 teaspoon
Butter, 6 tablespoons
Onion, chopped, 2
Lemon juice, 2 teaspoons
Beef stock, 1 cup
Port wine, 1 cup
Worcestershire sauce, 1 teaspoon
Bay leaf, 1

Garlic, crushed, 4 cloves
Mushrooms, sliced, 1 pound
Parsley, minced, ½ cup

Pastry:
Flour, sifted, 2 cups
Salt, 1 teaspoon
Double-acting baking powder,
    2 teaspoons
Butter, ½ cup
Eggs, 2
Vinegar, 2 tablespoons
Ice water, 4 tablespoons

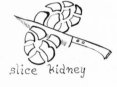

slice kidney

1. Cut the beef into 1″ cubes. Trim membranes from kidneys, slice; remove fat and white center core. Mix together the flour, salt, pepper, mace and mustard. Dredge the beef in it.

2. Heat 1 tablespoon butter in skillet and sauté onions until wilted. Remove. Add 4 tablespoons butter to skillet and brown meat on all sides. Remove and place in 3-quart casserole.

3. Add 1 tablespoon butter to skillet and sear kidneys quickly. Pour lemon juice over them and let sit for 1 minute. Remove to the casserole.

4. Add beef stock to skillet and bring to a boil, stirring to scrape up the browned bits. Stir in wine, Worcestershire sauce, bay leaf and garlic. Add to casserole the sautéed onions, the sliced mushrooms and parsley. Pour on sauce from skillet. Cover casserole and bake at 300° F. for 2 hours. Remove and cool until well chilled.

Pastry Procedure

1. Sift together flour, salt and baking powder. With a pastry blender, cut in butter. Beat 1 egg lightly and combine with vinegar and water. Stir into flour-butter mixture, adding more water if necessary to make a soft dough.

2. Form into a ball and roll out on a floured board, about ¼" thick and in a shape that is about ½" wider than the top of the casserole. Brush rim of the cooled casserole with an egg beaten with a little water. Place pastry loosely on top and seal the edges with the tines of a fork. Brush pastry top with remaining beaten egg.* Wrap casserole well and freeze.

Serving day: Cut 3 or 4 slits in frozen pastry top. Bake in 350° F. oven for 1½ hours. Serve with Eggplant Orégano.

seal edges
with fork

> **To serve without freezing, cut slits in pastry top.
> Bake at 350° F. for 1 hour.*

BEEF PIE WITH DUCHESS POTATO TOPPING

(4 or 6 servings)

Beef, round, 3 pounds	Apple cider, 1½ cups
Flour, 5 tablespoons	Tomato paste, 1 tablespoon
Salt, 2 teaspoons	Thyme, ½ teaspoon
Pepper, ½ teaspoon	Caraway seeds, 1 teaspoon
Garlic powder, ½ teaspoon	Small white onions, 2 cups
Butter, 3 tablespoons	(1 lb. can)
Garlic, crushed, 2 cloves	Duchess Potato (recipe follows)
Onion, chopped, 2	

1. Cut meat into 2" cubes. Mix flour with 1 teaspoon salt, ¼ teaspoon pepper, and garlic powder. Dredge meat in flour.

2. Heat 1 tablespoon of butter in Dutch oven. Sauté garlic and onion till golden. Remove. Add 2 tablespoons of butter and sear meat on all sides.

3. Put back garlic and onions. Add cider, tomato paste, 1 teaspoon salt, and ¼ teaspoon pepper. Cover and simmer for 2½ hours.

4. Add thyme, caraway seeds, and white onions. Cover and simmer for 30 minutes. Transfer to casserole.

5. Using a decorating tube or a spoon, cover casserole with Duchess Potatoes. Brush with melted butter.* Cool. Wrap and freeze.

Serving day: Bake, uncovered, in 400° F. oven for 1 hour.

To serve without freezing, bake, uncovered, at 400° F. for 45 minutes.

DUCHESS POTATOES

Potatoes, 4 medium sized	Pepper, ⅛ teaspoon
Butter, 2 tablespoons	Egg, 1
Cream, ⅓ cup	Chives, chopped, 3 tablespoons
Salt, 1 teaspoon	Poppy seeds, 1 tablespoon

Cook potatoes in boiling, salted water until tender. Drain. Peel and mash with potato masher. Heat butter and cream. Beat into potatoes with salt, pepper, egg, chives and poppy seeds.

COLD BRAISED BEEF IN WINE ASPIC
(10 to 12 servings)

Beef, rump or top round, 5 pounds (larded with pork)	Bay leaf, 1
Salt, 2 teaspoons	Lemon, 1 (juice and peel)
Black pepper, ½ teaspoon	Dry red wine, 2½ cups
Onion, chopped, 1 large	Olive oil, ½ cup
Carrot, sliced, 1	Meat drippings or bacon fat, 1 tablespoon
Celery, sliced, 2 stalks	Beef broth or water, ½ cup
Parsley, 4 sprigs	Veal knuckles, cracked, 2
Garlic, crushed, 2 cloves	Gelatin, 1 tablespoon
Thyme, 1 teaspoon	

1. Sprinkle meat with salt and pepper. Place it in a glass or earthenware bowl with the onion, carrot, celery, parsley, garlic, thyme, bay leaf, lemon juice and peel, wine and oil. Cover bowl and place in refrigerator for 12 to 24 hours, turning meat occasionally in marinade.

2. Remove meat and drain thoroughly, reserving the marinade. Pat dry. Heat fat in skillet and sear meat quickly on all sides.

3. Remove meat to dutch oven or casserole and deglaze skillet with ¼ cup broth, stirring in the browned bits. Pour this over the meat. Add the marinade and the veal knuckles. Cover and simmer for 4 hours on top of stove or in a 300° F. oven, turning the meat several times during the cooking.

4. Remove meat from liquid and refrigerate, covered. Strain liquid into a bowl and refrigerate until fat congeals (several hours or overnight).

5. Slice meat thinly and arrange in a rectangular mold or baking dish. Remove fat from liquid and reheat. Soften gelatin in ¼ cup broth and stir into hot liquid. Pour over meat. Cool.* Wrap mold and freeze.

Day before serving: Reheat frozen mold, covered, in 350° F. oven for 30 minutes. Cool and refrigerate in mold overnight to let aspic jell.

Serving day: Unmold on a platter before serving, or a few hours earlier, but keep refrigerated until serving time. Garnish with marinated baby beets or artichoke hearts.

> *To serve without freezing, refrigerate in mold until jelled. Serve cold as directed.

arrange meat in a rectangular dish

HOT BRAISED BEEF IN WINE

Follow recipe for Cold Braised Beef in Wine Aspic. Omit step of adding gelatin dissolved in ¼ cup broth.

Serving day: Reheat covered casserole in 350° F. oven for 45 minutes. Arrange meat on a hot platter and serve gravy separately. Serve with potato pancakes.

BOEUF BOURGUIGNON
(serves 6 to 8)

Beef round, 3 pounds,
  in 2″ cubes
Burgundy wine, 1½ cups
Brandy, 2 tablespoons
Salad oil, 2 tablespoons
Salt, 1 teaspoon
Pepper, ½ teaspoon
Thyme, ½ teaspoon
Parsley, 1 sprig
Bay leaf, 1

Butter, 6 tablespoons
Garlic, crushed, 2 cloves
Onion, chopped, 2 large
Carrot, chopped, 1
Flour, 4 rounded tablespoons
Tomato paste, 1 tablespoon
Beef broth, 1 cup
Tiny white onions, 1½ cups
  (1-lb. can)
Mushroom caps, ¾ pound

marinate beef

1. Marinate the beef for 2 hours in the wine, brandy, oil, salt, pepper, thyme, parsley and bay leaf. Turn occasionally.

2. Drain, reserving the marinade, removing parsley and bay leaf. Pat meat dry. Heat 3 tablespoons butter in heavy skillet. Brown the meat quickly on all sides. Remove meat to casserole.

3. Add 2 tablespoons of butter and sauté the garlic, onions, and carrot until lightly browned (about 5 or 6 minutes). Blend in flour and tomato paste. Add marinade and broth. Stir until mixture comes to a boil.

4. Pour over meat in casserole. Cover and cook in 350° F. oven for 2 hours.* Remove and cool. Wrap casserole and freeze.

5. Heat 1 tablespoon butter in skillet and sauté white onions till golden. Remove. Add mushroom caps and sauté for 2 minutes. Place onions and mushrooms in a freezer container and freeze.

Serving day: Heat casserole, uncovered, in 350° F. oven for 1½ hours. 30 minutes before serving, place onions and mushrooms on top and finish heating. Serve with potatoes au gratin.

> **To serve without freezing, bake for 30 minutes more. Sauté white onions and mushrooms as directed. Place on top of casserole and bake for 10 minutes more.*

HUNGARIAN GOULASH

(4 or 5 servings)

Boneless lean beef, cubed,
  2 pounds
Salt, pepper, and garlic powder
Butter, 3 tablespoons
Onions, sliced, 4
Carrots, sliced, 4
Celery, sliced, 4 stalks
Green peppers, shredded, 2
Garlic, crushed, 2 cloves

Paprika, 2 tablespoons
Tomato paste, 1 tablespoon
Flour, 3 tablespoons
Beef broth, 1½ cups
Salt, 2 teaspoons
Pepper, ½ teaspoon
Caraway seeds, 1 teaspoon
Sour cream, 1 cup
Sweet red peppers, shredded, 2

1. Sprinkle beef cubes with salt, pepper, and garlic powder. Heat 2 tablespoons of butter in deep skillet and brown meat quickly. Remove.

2. Heat remaining butter in pan and add onions, carrots, celery, green peppers and garlic. Cook over moderate heat for 5 minutes, stirring occasionally. Stir in paprika and cook for another minute. Blend in tomato paste and flour. Stir in broth and bring to a boil. Add meat, salt, pepper, and caraway seeds. Cover and cook slowly for 2½ hours.

3. Remove the meat to a freezer container. Strain the sauce, pressing the vegetables through a sieve, and pour over the meat.* Cool. Freeze.

Serving day: Reheat in double boiler for about 1 hour. Before serving, stir in red peppers and sour cream and heat through. (Do not boil.) Serve with rice, noodles or polenta.

> *To serve without freezing, reheat for 20 minutes. Stir in red peppers and sour cream and heat through. Do not boil.

press vegetables through sieve

BOEUF STROGANOFF

(serves 8)

Beef, top sirloin or top round,
  3 pounds
Lemon juice, ½ cup
Butter, 6 tablespoons
Onions, finely chopped, 2 large
Mushrooms, sliced, 1 pound
  (4 cups)
Flour, 5 tablespoons

Tomato paste, 1 rounded
  teaspoon
Ground dill, ½ teaspoon
Salt, 1½ teaspoons
Pepper, ¼ teaspoon
Beef broth, 1½ cups
Sour cream, 2 cups
Dill seeds, 2 teaspoons
Caraway seeds, 1 teaspoon

1. Cut meat into strips about 2″ long and ½″ wide. Place in bowl and cover with lemon juice. Leave for 30 minutes. Drain.

2. Heat 2 tablespoons butter in Dutch oven. Brown meat quickly on all sides. Remove.

3. Heat 2 tablespoons butter in same pan and cook onions until soft and golden. Add remaining butter and cook mushrooms for 3 minutes, stirring occasionally. Blend in flour, tomato paste, ground dill, salt and pepper. Stir in broth gradually, and bring to a boil. Add meat to sauce.* Cool. Pack in container. Freeze.

Serving day: Heat in double boiler for 2½ hours. Before serving, stir in sour cream, dill seeds and caraway seed and cook until heated through. (Do not boil.) Serve with noodles mixed with butter and chopped parsley.

> *To serve without freezing, simmer for 1 hour. Stir in sour cream, dill and caraway seeds and heat as directed.*

cut meat into strips

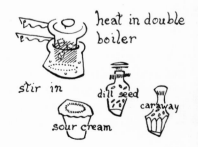

heat in double boiler

stir in

sour cream

dill seed

caraway

STUFFED LEG OF LAMB WITH BARBECUE SAUCE

(serves 6 to 8)

Whole leg of lamb, 6 to 7 pounds, boned. Have the butcher remove the bone from the lamb, leaving it intact, with a neat cavity for stuffing, and secured at one end with butcher's twine.

STUFFING

White bread, 2 slices
Cream, ½ cup
Butter, 2 tablespoons
Onion, chopped, 1
Mushrooms, sliced, 2 cups
  (½ pound)
Ham, ground, ½ pound
Veal, ground, ¼ pound

Canned water chestnuts, sliced,
  ½ cup
Egg, beaten, 1
Garlic, crushed, 2 cloves
Salt, ¼ teaspoon
Pepper, ⅛ teaspoon
Dill seeds, ½ teaspoon

BARBECUE SAUCE

(3 cups)

Butter, ½ pound
Catsup, 1 cup
Tomato paste, 2 heaping
  tablespoons
Tarragon vinegar, 3 tablespoons
  (or wine vinegar with ½
  teaspoon dried tarragon)
Salt, 2 teaspoons
Lemon juice, 2 tablespoons
Worcestershire sauce,
  2 tablespoons
Onion, chopped, 2 small
Garlic, crushed, 3 cloves

Dry mustard, 2 teaspoons
Paprika, 2 teaspoons
Pepper, ¼ teaspoon
Brown sugar, 2 teaspoons

Flour, 1 tablespoon
Water, 2½ cups

1. Soak bread in cream. Heat butter and sauté onions and mushrooms until lightly browned. To the bread, add the onions, mushrooms, ground meat, water chestnuts, beaten egg and seasoning and blend thoroughly. Stretch the lamb cavity open and pack in stuffing. Sew up the ends or tie with string.

stuff lamb   sew up ends

2. Combine all sauce ingredients in a saucepan. Simmer for ½ hour, stirring occasionally. Pour 1 cup into freezer container and freeze.

3. Place the stuffed lamb in roasting pan and spoon sauce over it. Roast, uncovered, at 300° F. Allow 20 minutes to the pound. Baste every 30 minutes with the sauce. After 1 hour, turn the lamb over and begin basting the other side until time is up.* Remove lamb and cool in refrigerator.

4. Blend 1 tablespoon of flour with the pan drippings over a low heat, stirring till smooth. Add 2½ cups of water and bring to a boil. Simmer for a few minutes. Cool. Remove thread or strings from lamb. Wrap in foil and freeze. Pour gravy into a container and freeze.

Night before serving: Transfer wrapped lamb, gravy, and the cup of barbecue sauce to refrigerator.

Serving day: 2½ hours before serving, remove wrappings from lamb and heat in covered roaster in 350° oven. Half an hour before serving, reheat the cup of barbecue sauce and baste the lamb. Roast, uncovered, for remaining time.

Remove congealed fat from gravy and heat. Slice the lamb at the table and serve the gravy separately. Serve with Barley Pilaf.

*To serve without freezing, roast for 1 more hour, basting twice. Make gravy as directed, skimming off fat.

LAMB AVGOLEMONO
(6 servings)

Lean shoulder of lamb, boned
   and cubed in 3" pieces,
   3 pounds
Salt, pepper and garlic powder
Oil, 2 tablespoons
Butter, 2 tablespoons
Onion, chopped, 3
Flour, 2 tablespoons
Water, ½ cup

White wine, ½ cup
Fresh dill, minced, 2 tablespoons
Fresh parsley, minced,
   2 tablespoons
Salt, ¾ teaspoon
Celery, 1 bunch
Zucchini, 3
Egg yolks, 4
Lemon juice, 6 tablespoons

1. Sprinkle lamb with salt, pepper and garlic powder. Heat oil and brown meat on all sides. Remove.

2. Add butter and cook onion over moderate heat until wilted. Blend in flour. Add water and cook, stirring until thick and smooth. Add wine. Put back meat with dill, parsley, and salt and simmer, covered, for 1 hour.

3. Slice celery diagonally into 1" pieces and chop half the leaves. Scrape zucchini but do not peel. Slice diagonally into 2" pieces.

4. Add zucchini, celery and chopped leaves to stew. Cover and cook for 10 minutes.* Cool. Pour into a freezer container and freeze.

Serving day: Reheat over low heat for about 45 minutes or until hot. When ready to serve, beat egg yolks until thick. Beat in lemon juice, 1 tablespoon at a time. Gradually stir in 1 cup of hot liquid from stew. Slowly pour egg mixture into stew, stirring into hot sauce until well mixed.

Serve with Rice Pilaf mixed with canned chick peas which have been sautéed with chopped onion.

*To serve without freezing, cook for 15 more minutes. Stir in egg-lemon mixture as directed.

stir in hot liquid
while beating

GIGOT en CROUTE
Leg of Lamb in Crust

(serves 8 to 10)

Leg of lamb, 5 to 6 pounds
Salt, pepper and garlic powder
Butter, 3 tablespoons
Garlic, crushed, 2 cloves
Onion, chopped, 1 large
Ground veal, ¾ pound
Ground pork, ¼ pound
Walnuts, toasted and chopped,
    ½ cup
Celery, chopped, 1 stalk
Parsley, minced, 2 tablespoons

Salt, ½ teaspoon
Pepper, ⅛ teaspoon
Rosemary, ¼ teaspoon
Egg white, 1
Onion, sliced, 1
Water, ½ cup
Red wine, 1 cup
Potato flour, 1 teaspoon
Chicken broth, 2 cups
Brandy, 2 tablespoons

PASTRY

Flour, 6 cups
Salt, 2 teaspoons
Double-acting baking powder,
    4 teaspoons
Butter, 1 cup
Lard, ½ cup

Egg yolks, 3
Vinegar, ⅓ cup
Ice water, ⅓ cup
Egg white, 1
Egg, 1

1. Have the butcher bone the lamb completely, leaving it whole with a neat cavity for stuffing, secured at one end with butcher's twine. Remove fat and sprinkle lamb inside and out with salt, pepper and garlic powder.

2 Heat 1 tablespoon of butter and sauté garlic and chopped onion until wilted. Combine with ground meat, walnuts, celery, parsley, seasoning and egg white. Mix together thoroughly. Stuff lamb pocket with filling. Fold flaps up over stuffing and tie up securely with string.

3. In a roasting pan, place sliced onions and water. Place lamb on top of onions (without a rack), rub it with 2 tablespoons softened butter and baste with 2 tablespoons wine. Roast at 375° F. for 15 minutes. Reduce heat to 350° F., baste with 2 tablespoons wine, and roast for 1 hour and 20 minutes, basting at intervals with remaining wine. Remove from pan and cool.

4. Blend potato flour into the pan juices. Gradually add broth and cook over low heat, stirring until thickened and smooth. Add brandy. Cool. Remove strings from cooled lamb.* Wrap and freeze. Pour cooled gravy into container and freeze.

5. Combine flour, salt and baking powder in a large bowl. Make a well in the center and put into it the butter, lard, egg yolks, vinegar and ice water. (With fingers) work center ingredients into a smooth paste. Gradually work in the flour until dough is smooth. Form into a ball.* Wrap and freeze.

Day before: Transfer lamb and dough to refrigerator to thaw, wrapped, for 24 hours.

Serving day: 2 hours and 45 minutes before serving, remove lamb and dough from refrigerator. Let stand, unwrapped, at room temperature for 30 minutes.

Roll out dough in a circle ½" thick and large enough to wrap lamb completely. Place lamb in center, top side down. Wrap pastry around meat. Trim excess and seal edges with egg white. Place lamb, seam side down, on a cooky sheet.(1) Brush top and sides with an egg, lightly beaten with a little water. Make slits for steam to escape.

Bake at 375° F. for 15 minutes. Reduce heat to 350° F. and bake for 2 hours. Reheat frozen gravy over low heat until hot. Serve the lamb on a hot platter and slice at the table. Serve the gravy separately. Serve with Broccoli Ring and Flageolet Salad.

Note: (1) Optional. At this stage, excess pastry can be thinly rolled out and cut into rounds or triangles to decorate top. Attach by brushing bottom of cut-outs with egg white and pressing edges with a fork to pastry top.

*To serve without freezing, follow directions for rolling out dough, wrapping lamb and baking, but reduce final baking time (in 350° oven) to one hour.

lamb on pastry

wrap pastry around meat... trim excess

brush scraps with egg-white and attach to pastry

INDIAN LAMB CURRY

(serves 4 to 6)

Flour, 3 tablespoons
Salt, 2 teaspoons
Cayenne pepper, ¼ teaspoon
Curry powder, 2 tablespoons
Lamb, leg or shoulder, in
    1″ cubes, 3 pounds
Butter, ¼ pound
Onions, chopped, 3
Celery, chopped, 3 stalks
Garlic, crushed, 3 cloves

Beef broth, 1 cup
Cream, ½ cup
Tomato paste, 1 tablespoon
Lemon juice, 2 tablespoons
Green apples, finely chopped,
    4 (or tart red apples)
Golden seedless raisins,
    4 tablespoons
Currant jelly, 2 tablespoons
Grated coconut, 4 tablespoons

1. Combine flour with salt, pepper and curry powder. Dredge meat in the seasoned flour.

2. Melt 1½ tablespoons butter in Dutch oven. Sauté onions, celery, and garlic for 15 minutes. Remove vegetables. Add remaining butter to same pan and sear meat on all sides. Remove meat.

3. Add 1 cup of broth to pan. Bring to a boil, scraping up the drippings. Return meat and vegetables to pan. Add cream and tomato paste. Cover and simmer for 30 minutes.

4. Add lemon juice, apples, raisins, currant jelly, and grated coconut. Cover and simmer for 1 hour.* Cool. Pour into container and freeze.

Serving day: Heat in double boiler or over moderate heat for 1 hour or until thoroughly hot. Serve with rice, chutney, grated fresh coconut (or canned), chopped green pepper, sliced kumquats, chopped cucumber and chopped red onions mixed with yogurt and toasted cumin seed, diced avocado sprinkled with lemon juice, sliced toasted almonds and whatever else appeals to you.

*To serve without freezing, simmer for 20 to 30 minutes more.

QUENELLES de VEAU WITH MUSHROOM-MADEIRA SAUCE
Veal Dumplings

(about 36)

Water, 1 cup	Boneless veal, ground,
Salt, 1½ teaspoons	1½ pounds (2¼ cups)
Butter, 10 tablespoons	White pepper, ½ teaspoon
Sifted flour, 1 cup	Dry mustard, ½ teaspoon
Eggs, 6	Paprika, ½ teaspoon
	Ground dill, ½ teaspoon

1. Heat water and salt in saucepan until boiling. Add 4 tablespoons butter and slowly melt. Remove from heat and add flour all at once, stirring with a wooden spoon to blend thoroughly. Put back over moderate heat and beat vigorously until mixture leaves the side of the pan and forms a smooth, shiny ball. Transfer to mixing bowl.

2. Add 4 eggs, one at a time, beating thoroughly after each addition. Add ground veal and seasoning. Beat for 6 minutes at high speed, pushing the mixture into the beaters occasionally with a rubber spataula. Cream remaining 6 tablespoons butter with a wooden spoon and gradually beat into mixture. Beat in remaining 2 eggs, one at a time. Spread mixture on flat pan and chill in freezer for 15 minutes (not directly on freezing coils), or in refrigerator for 6 hours or overnight.

3. Wet hands with cold water and form mixture into small sausage-shaped quenelles. In a large roasting pan, bring to a boil 4″ chicken broth or salted water. Reduce heat to a simmer and carefully slip in quenelles. Poach, uncovered, for 10 minutes. Gently, turn over and poach 5 minutes longer. Remove carefully with a slotted spoon and drain on a towel.* When cool and firm, carefully place on a flat surface and place in freezer. When frozen firm, pack in a container. Return to freezer.

roll on floured board into sausage shapes

poach for 15 minutes

on baking dish

Serving day: Place frozen quenelles on a greased baking and serving dish. Bake, covered, at 350° F. for 25 to 30 minutes. Pour reheated Mushroom-Madeira Sauce over dish and serve very hot. Serve with whole tomatoes, scooped out and stuffed with cold rice mixed with chopped scallions, parsley, tomato pulp, lemon juice, oil and salt and pepper.

*To serve without freezing, heat, covered, at 350° F. for 10 minutes. Pour on sauce.

MUSHROOM-MADEIRA SAUCE

(about 2 cups)

Butter, 3 tablespoons
Shallots or green onions,
  chopped, 2 tablespoons
Mushrooms, sliced, ½ pound

Brown sauce, 1½ cups
  (see index)
Madeira wine, ½ cup
Fresh parsley, minced,
  1 tablespoon

Heat butter and sauté shallots and mushrooms for 4 to 5 minutes. Add brown sauce and bring to a boil. Simmer for 5 minutes. Cool and pack in container.

Serving day: Reheat sauce until boiling. Before serving, stir in Madeira and bring to the boiling point but do not boil. Stir in parsley and serve.

Note: In place of long-cooked brown sauce, you may substitute the following:

QUICK BROWN SAUCE

Meat drippings or butter,
  1½ tablespoons
Flour, 1½ tablespoons

Beef stock, 2 cups
Thyme, ⅛ teaspoon

Heat fat in saucepan. Blend in flour and cook over low heat, stirring occasionally, until flour is browned. Gradually add stock, and bring to a boil, stirring constantly. Cover and simmer for 30 minutes until reduced to 1½ cups. Skim off fat and use.

ITALIAN VEAL ROLLS

(5 servings)

Dried mushrooms, 4
Veal Scallopine, 10 slices
  (about 1½ pounds)
Salt, pepper and garlic powder
Butter, 3 tablespoons
Shallots or scallions, chopped
  ¼ cup
Celery, chopped, 1 stalk
Parsley, minced, ½ cup
Pignole nuts, chopped, ¼ cup
  (1½ ounces)
Parmesan cheese, grated,
  2 tablespoons

Boiled ham, thinly sliced,
  ¼ pound
Oil, 2 tablespoons
Garlic, crushed, 3 cloves
Onions, chopped, ½ cup
Flour, 1 tablespoon
Chicken broth, 1 cup
White wine, ¼ cup
Salt, ½ teaspoon
Fresh mushrooms, coarsely
  chopped, ½ pound

1. Soak dried mushrooms in ¼ cup of warm water for 30 minutes. Place veal between 2 sheets of wax paper and pound thin with a wooden mallet or flat side of heavy knife. Sprinkle with salt, pepper and garlic powder.

2. Melt 1 tablespoon of butter and sauté shallots and celery over moderate heat, until wilted. Mix in parsley, nuts and cheese. Drain mushrooms, reserving liquid. Chop and add to mixture.

3. Place a slice of ham, trimmed to fit, on each slice of veal. Put a heaping tablespoon of mixture on top of ham and roll up veal. Fold up ends to close in stuffing and tie up rolls with string. Heat oil in skillet and brown rolls quickly on all sides. Remove from pan to shallow casserole.

4. Add remaining 2 tablespoons butter to pan and sauté garlic and onions until wilted. Blend in flour. Gradually add broth and cook over low heat, stirring until thickened. Add wine, reserved dried mushroom liquid, salt, and chopped fresh mushrooms. Simmer for 5 minutes. Remove strings from veal rolls and spoon on sauce.* Cool. Wrap up casserole and freeze.

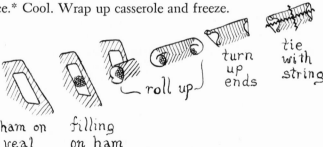

ham on veal   filling on ham   roll up   turn up ends   tie with string

Serving day: Heat casserole, covered, at 375° F. for 1½ hours. Serve with fettucini mixed with butter and grated cheese.

To serve without freezing, heat covered casserole at 375° F. for 45 minutes.

PAUPIETTES de VEAU
Stuffed Veal Rolls

(6 servings)

pound veal

Dried mushrooms, 6
Veal Scallopine, 12 slices
  (about 2 pounds)
Salt, pepper and garlic powder
Butter, 5 tablespoons
Onion, sliced, 1
Chicken livers, ½ pound
Fresh mushrooms, chopped,
  ½ pound (2 cups)
Chestnuts, peeled and chopped,
  ½ cup (¼ pound in the shell)

Fresh parsley, finely chopped,
  ¼ cup
Salt, ¾ teaspoon
Pepper, ⅛ teaspoon
Oil, 2 tablespoons
Flour, 1 tablespoon
Chicken broth, 1½ cups
Paprika, ¼ teaspoon
Sour cream, 2 tablespoons
Almonds, slivered and toasted,
  3 tablespoons

1. Soak dried mushrooms in ¼ cup of warm water for 30 minutes. Place veal between 2 sheets of wax paper and pound thin with a wooden mallet or flat side of heavy knife. Sprinkle with salt, pepper and garlic powder.

2. Heat 2 tablespoons of butter and sauté onion over moderate heat. Add livers and brown quickly on all sides. (Do not overcook.) Remove onions and liver from pan. Add 2 tablespoons of butter and sauté mushrooms for 3 or 4 minutes. Chop livers and onions and mix with sautéed mushrooms, chestnuts, parsley, salt and pepper.

3. Put a heaping tablespoonful of mixture on top of veal slices and roll up. Fold up ends to close in stuffing and tie up rolls with string. Heat oil in skillet and brown rolls quickly on all sides. Remove from pan to shallow casserole.

4. Heat remaining tablespoon of butter in pan and blend in flour. Gradually add broth and cook over low heat, stirring until thick. Add to sauce, dried mushrooms with their liquid and

paprika. Remove strings from rolls and spoon on sauce.* Cool. Wrap and freeze.

Serving day: Bake, covered, in 375° F. oven for 1 hour and 20 minutes. Stir in sour cream and heat through for another 10 minutes. Sprinkle with almonds and serve with wild rice.

> *To serve without freezing, bake, covered, at 375° F. for about 45 minutes and stir in sour cream.

have veal shanks
cut 3 inches long

OSSO BUCO
(4 servings)

Veal shanks, 3″ long, 4	Garlic, crushed, 1 clove
Salt, pepper, and powdered garlic	Salt, ½ teaspoon
Flour, 2 tablespoons	Pepper, ¼ teaspoon
Butter, 2 tablespoons	Basil, ½ teaspoon
Olive oil, 2 tablespoons	Chicken or beef broth, 1 cup
Carrots, chopped, 2	Tomato paste, 2 tablespoons
Onions, chopped, 2	Lemon rind, grated, 1 teaspoon
Celery chopped, 2 stalks	Parsley, minced, 2 tablespoons

1. Sprinkle meat with salt, pepper and powdered garlic. Dredge with flour. Heat butter and oil in heavy skillet and sear meat on all sides until well browned.

2. Add carrots, onion, celery, garlic, salt, pepper, and basil. Cover and simmer for 30 minutes. Add broth and tomato paste. Cover and simmer for another 30 minutes.

3. Remove meat to freezer container. Purée sauce and vegetables in electric blender or through sieve and pour over meat.* Freeze.

Serving day: Reheat in double boiler for 1½ hours. Before serving, stir in lemon rind and parsley. Serve with Risotto Milanese or fettucini noodles mixed with butter and grated cheese.

> *To serve without freezing, simmer for 30 minutes. Stir in lemon rind and parsley.

BLANQUETTE OF VEAL

(4 or 6 servings)

Water, 4 cups
Celery, sliced with leaves, 2 stalks
Carrots, sliced, 2
Onions, 2
Parsley, minced, 2 teaspoons
Bay leaf, 1
Cloves, 2 (stuck in carrot)
Peppercorns, 6
Thyme, ½ teaspoon
Salt, 1 teaspoon
Cayenne pepper, ¼ teaspoon
Boneless veal, cubed, 2 pounds

Butter, 6 tablespoons
Canned small white onions,
    drained, 20 (½ of 1 lb. can)
Small mushroom caps, 2 cups
    (½ pound)
Flour, 3 tablespoons
Salt, 1 teaspoon
Paprika, ⅛ teaspoon
Egg yolks, 2
Heavy cream, 1 cup
Lemon juice, 2 teaspoons

1. Place water, celery, carrots, onions, parsley, bay leaf, cloves, peppercorns, thyme, salt and cayenne in saucepan and bring to a boil. Add meat. Cover and simmer for 1 hour. Remove from heat and strain stock.

2. Heat 2 tablespoons butter in heavy skillet and sauté onions till lightly browned. Remove. Add 1 tablespoon butter to pan and sauté mushrooms for 4 minutes. Remove.

3. Add 3 tablespoons of butter to pan and heat. Blend in flour. Stir in 2 cups of veal stock. Add salt and paprika. Cook until smooth and thickened. Add onions, mushrooms, and veal to sauce.* Cool. Pour into freezer containers and freeze.

Serving day: Heat in double boiler for 2 hours or in 350° F. oven for 1½ hours. Before serving, beat egg yolks with cream. Add to sauce and heat through. Stir in lemon juice. Serve with rice or buttered noodles mixed with poppy seeds.

*To serve without freezing, simmer for 45 minutes.
Add egg yolks, cream and lemon juice as directed.*

beat egg yolks
with cream,

add to sauce

add lemon juice

VEAL SCALLOPINE WITH CHESTNUTS

(4 or 5 servings)

Veal scallops, 1¼ pounds
Dried mushrooms, 5 or 6
Flour, ¼ cup
Salt, 1 teaspoon
Pepper, ¼ teaspoon
Paprika, ½ teaspoon
Butter, 2 tablespoons
Oil, 2 tablespoons
Garlic, crushed, 2 cloves
Shallots or white onions,
   coarsely chopped, 3 or 4

Chicken or beef broth, 1 cup
Tomato paste, 1 teaspoon
Salt, ½ teaspoon
Pepper, ⅛ teaspoon
Basil, ½ teaspoon
Tarragon, ½ teaspoon
Marsala, ¼ cup
Dry white wine, ¼ cup
Boiled chestnuts, in large pieces,
   1 cup (½ pound)
Sour cream, 1 cup

1. Pound veal scallops with wooden mallet or with the side of a heavy knife until very thin. Cut into pieces about 2" x 3". Cut up mushrooms and soak in ¼ cup water for 30 minutes.

2. Mix flour with salt, pepper and paprika. Dip veal into flour and shake off excess. Heat butter and oil. Cook garlic for 1 minute. Sauté meat over a brisk fire until golden brown on both sides. Remove meat from pan.

3. Add shallots or onions to pan and cook over low heat until softened. Add broth and cook for a few minutes, scraping up the browned bits from bottom of pan. Add tomato paste, mushrooms with their liquid, seasonings, marsala and wine. Stir until well blended. Remove from heat and stir in meat and chestnuts.* Cool. Pack in containers. Freeze.

Serving day: Heat in double boiler or in heavy saucepan over low heat for about 45 minutes or until very hot. Stir in sour cream and heat through but do not boil. Serve with noodles mixed with butter and paprika.

To serve without freezing, simmer for 15 minutes. Stir in sour cream and heat through.

pound veal with the side of a heavy knife

SWEET AND SOUR PORK

(8 servings)

Boneless loin of pork,
  in 1″ cubes, 2 pounds
Sherry, 2 tablespoons
Soy sauce, ¼ cup
Cornstarch, 3 tablespoons
Flour, 1 tablespoon
Oil, 6 tablespoons
Garlic, crushed, 2 cloves
Pineapple chunks, 1 pound,
  4½-oz. can

Cider vinegar, ½ cup
Monosodium glutamate,
  ½ teaspoon
Pepper, dash
Cold water, 3 tablespoons
Carrots, 2
Green peppers, cut in chunks, 6
White onions, quartered, 4
Oil for frying, 2 cups

cut carrots in 1 inch slices

1. Marinate pork for 1 hour in a mixture of the sherry, 2 tablespoons of soy sauce, 2 tablespoons of cornstarch and 1 tablespoon of flour.

2. Heat 1 tablespoon of oil and cook garlic over moderate heat for 1 minute. Drain pineapple and add juice to skillet. (Should be 1 cup.) Add vinegar, remaining soy sauce, MSG and pepper and bring to a boil. Dissolve 1 tablespoon of cornstarch in water and add to sauce. Cook for ½ minute. Reserve sauce.

3. Cut carrots in 1″ lengths. Cover with boiling salted water and boil for 8 minutes. Drain. Heat 5 tablespoons of oil in a large skillet and sauté peppers, onions and carrots for 3 minutes. (You may have to do this in 2 installments to fit in all the vegetables.) Add pineapple chunks and cook for 1 minute. Pour into two 1-pint freezer containers and freeze.

4. Place 2 cups of oil in a heavy pot and bring to a boil. Add pork and deep-fry until crisp and golden (about 7 to 8 minutes). Remove pork with a slotted spoon and drain on absorbent paper. Stir into sauce* and cool quickly. Place in freezer container and freeze.

Serving day: Reheat in double boiler or over very low heat until hot (about 45 minutes). Add frozen sautéed vegetables and cook until thoroughly hot. Do not overcook. Serve with rice.

Note: Fry pork by browning in very hot temperature (400° F.) for 1 minute and then reducing heat slightly so that the meat doesn't burn and can cook all the way through. All the meat will not fit in the pan at one time. Fry in several batches.

> **To serve without freezing, heat for 15 minutes. Combine with sautéed vegetables and serve.*

CHINESE SPARERIBS WITH KUMQUATS

(serves 4 to 6)

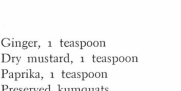

deep-fry pork until golden

Spareribs, 6 pounds	Ginger, 1 teaspoon
Soy sauce, ½ cup	Dry mustard, 1 teaspoon
Chicken broth, ½ cup	Paprika, 1 teaspoon
Dark corn syrup, ½ cup	Preserved kumquats,
Sherry, ½ cup	1 9-ounce bottle
Garlic, crushed, 6 cloves	

1. Place spareribs on rack in a flat roasting pan. Roast at 325° F. for 1 hour and 15 minutes.

2. Meanwhile, combine soy sauce, broth, corn syrup, sherry, garlic, ginger, mustard and paprika in a saucepan and simmer for 3 or 4 minutes. Reserve.

3. Remove meat from pan and cut into individual ribs. Pour off fat in pan and put back ribs without the rack. Spoon on sauce, coating ribs thoroughly. Bake at 375° F. for 40 minutes, basting and turning occasionally.* Remove from pan and cool. Place in freezer container or bag and freeze.

Serving day: Slice kumquats, removing pits. Put frozen ribs in baking pan and pour over the kumquats and syrup. Cover and bake at 375° F. for 25 to 30 minutes.

> **To serve without freezing, add sliced kumquats and syrup and bake 10 more minutes.*

CASSOULET

(serves 8 or 10)

Dried white beans (White Kidney or Great Northern), 1 pound
Duck, 4½ to 5 lbs., 1
Salt, pepper and garlic powder
Orange, quartered, 1
Onion, quartered, 1
Apricot preserves, 3 tablespoons
Garlic, crushed, 6 cloves
Onions, chopped, 4
Flour, 1 tablespoon
Chicken broth, 3 cups
Water, 1 cup
Tomato sauce, 1 cup
Salt pork, diced, ½ pound
Pork rind, in one piece, ½ pound

Parsley, 4 sprigs
Carrot, 1
Celery, 1 stalk with leaves
Bay leaf, 1
Leaf thyme, 1 teaspoon
Whole cloves, 2
Black peppercorns, 5
Polish garlic sausage, 1¼ pounds
Pork loin, boned and cubed, 1¼ pounds
Leg of lamb, boned and cubed, 1¼ pounds
Dry white wine, 1 cup
Salt, ½ teaspoon
Pepper, ⅛ teaspoon
Parsley, minced, ½ cup

1. Cover beans with cold water and soak overnight, or boil 2 minutes covered and let soak 1 hour. Drain.

2. Remove as much fat as possible from duck and sprinkle inside and out with salt, pepper and garlic powder. Fill cavity with quartered orange and onion. Roast duck on a rack in 325° F. oven for 2 hours, pricking once or twice to let fat run out. Spread top of duck with apricot preserves and roast in 400° F. oven for 15 minutes more.

3. Heat 1 tablespoon of duck drippings in skillet and sauté 3 crushed garlic cloves and 2 chopped onions until soft. Blend in flour. Gradually add 2 cups of broth and cook over low heat, stirring until thickened. Add water and ½ cup of tomato sauce and heat through. Reserve.

duck   salt pork   sausage

4. Cover salt pork and rind with cold water. Bring to a boil and simmer for 2 minutes. Drain. Tie up in a cheesecloth bag parsley sprigs, carrot, celery, bay leaf, ½ teaspoon thyme, cloves and peppercorns. Place drained beans in a large heavy pot with bag of herbs, duck neck, duck giblets cut up, salt pork and rind. Add reserved sauce, cover and simmer for 30 minutes. Add sausage (in one piece) and simmer for 30 minutes more.

5. Heat 1 tablespoon of duck drippings in skillet and sauté remaining garlic and onions until soft. Remove. Add 1 tablespoon of duck drippings to skillet. Brown cubed pork and lamb on all sides. Put back sautéed garlic and onions and add remaining cup of broth, the wine, ½ cup of tomato sauce, ½ teaspoon thyme, salt and pepper. Cover and simmer for 1 hour.

6. When beans are finished, remove bag of herbs, sausage, duck neck and pork rind. Discard bag and neck, slice sausage and dice pork rind. Add sausage to meats. Cut up duck into small portions. Add to meats.

7. In a 5- or 6-quart casserole, arrange on bottom a layer of beans, a sprinkling of minced parsley, a layer of combined meats and juices, then a layer of beans and parsley. Continue adding layers until dish is full, ending with beans. Top with diced pork rind.* Cool, wrap and freeze.

Serving day: Bake, covered, at 350° F. for 2½ hours. Uncover and bake for 30 minutes more. Serve with green salad garnished with marinated raw mushrooms and zucchini à la grecque.

To serve without freezing, bake uncovered at 350° F. for 1½ hours, uncover and continue baking for 30 minutes more.

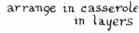

arrange in casserole
in layers

wrap herbs
in cheesecloth

pork rind
beans
meats
parsley
beans
meats
parsley
beans

LASAGNE

(serves 8 to 10)

Olive oil, 2 tablespoons
Onions, chopped, 2
Garlic, crushed, 2 cloves
Ground lean beef, 1 pound
Ground veal, ½ pound
Italian hot sausage, ¼ pound
Canned whole tomatoes with
 liquid, 3½ cups (1 lb. 12-oz
 can)
Tomato purée, 3½ cups
 (1 lb. 12-oz can)
Tomato paste, 1 small can
 (6 oz.)

Beef broth, 1 cup
Salt, 2 teaspoons
Pepper, ¼ teaspoon
Sugar, 1 teaspoon
Lasagne noodles, 1 pound
Eggs, 2
Ricotta cheese, 1 pound
Grated Parmesan cheese, ½ cup
Mozzarella cheese, thinly sliced,
 1 pound
Basil, 1 tablespoon
Orégano, 2 tablespoons

1. Heat oil in Dutch oven. Add onions and cook till soft and golden. Add garlic and meat and sauté for 15 minutes, stirring occasionally. Add tomatoes, tomato purée, tomato paste, broth, salt, pepper, and sugar. Simmer for 2 hours. (Makes 8 cups of sauce.)

2. Boil noodles for 15 minutes, in large kettle of actively boiling salted water. Drain. Rinse with cold water.

3. Beat eggs till foamy. Mix with ricotta.

4. Spoon sauce over bottom of baking dish. Line with lasagne, dot with ricotta, grated cheese, mozzarella, sauce, and a sprinkling of basil and orégano. Repeat this process until all ingredients are used. Top with sauce, mozzarella, and grated cheese.* Wrap in foil. Freeze.

arrange in casserole in layers

Serving day: Bake, uncovered, at 375° F. for 1 hour.

*To serve without freezing, bake, uncovered, 30 minutes.

grated cheese
mozzarella
sauce
herbs
ricotta
lasagne
herbs
sauce
all cheeses
lasagne
sauce

STUFFED CABBAGE LEAVES
(4 servings)

Large cabbage leaves, 8
Ground beef, 1 pound
Cooked rice, 1 cup
Garlic, crushed, 1 clove

Onion, finely chopped, 1
Parsley, minced, 2 tablespoons
Salt, 1 teaspoon
Black pepper, ⅛ teaspoon
Cayenne, ⅛ teaspoon

SAUCE

Butter, 2 tablespoons
Garlic, crushed, 1 clove
Onion, chopped, 2 medium
Whole tomatoes, 4 cups with
    liquid (one 2 lb. 3-oz. can)
Beef broth, ½ cup
Brown sugar, ½ cup
Tarragon vinegar, 1 tablespoon

Lemon juice, 2 tablespoons
Salt, 1½ teaspoons
Black pepper, ¼ teaspoon
Bay leaf, 1
Thyme, ¼ teaspoon
Caraway seeds, 1 teaspoon
Honey, 2 tablespoons
Sour cream, 2 tablespoons

1. Cook cabbage leaves in boiling salted water for 5 minutes. Drain and cut out thick center spine.

2. Combine meat, rice, garlic, onion, parsley and seasonings. Place a generous compact spoonful on each leaf. Fold the leaf around the filling to make a meat package. Secure with toothpicks. Place in casserole, folded side down.

3. Heat butter and sauté garlic and onions until golden. Add tomatoes, broth, sugar, vinegar, lemon juice, salt, pepper, bay leaf, thyme and caraway seeds. Simmer for 10 minutes. Spoon sauce over cabbage rolls. Bake covered casserole at 350° F. for 1 hour.* Cool, wrap and freeze.

Serving day: Uncover casserole and heat at 350° F. for 1 hour. Thirty minutes before serving, stir in honey and sour cream.

*To serve without freezing, uncover, stir in honey and sour cream. Bake 30 minutes more.

cut out center spine   fold leaf around filling

PICADILLO
Cuban Hash
(6 to 8 servings)

Chopped beef, 2 pounds
Sherry, 1 cup
Salt, 2½ teaspoons
Black pepper, 1 teaspoon
Oil, 5 tablespoons
Garlic, crushed, 3 cloves
Onions, chopped, 2
Green pepper, chopped, 1
Pitted olives, ripe or stuffed,
    sliced, ½ cup
Capers, ¼ cup

Bay leaf, 1
Ground cumin, 1/16 teaspoon
Orégano, 1/16 teaspoon
Seedless raisins, ½ cup
Pignole nuts, ¼ cup
Canned whole tomatoes, drained
    and crushed, 2 cups (1 lb.
    12 oz. can)
Tomato sauce, 1 cup (8-oz. can)
Sherry, 1½ cup

1. Mix beef with ½ cup sherry, salt and pepper. Let stand at room temperature for 1 hour.

2. Heat 3 tablespoons of oil in heavy Dutch oven. Sauté garlic for 1 minute. Add meat and sauté lightly. Remove from pan. Add 2 tablespoons of oil to pan. Sauté onions, peppers, and olives until lightly browned.

3. Stir in meat, capers, seasoning, raisins, pignole nuts, tomatoes, and tomato sauce. Simmer, uncovered, for 1 hour.* Cool. Pack in freezer container. Freeze.

Serving day: Reheat in double boiler or over low heat for about 45 minutes until thoroughly hot. Before serving, stir in ½ cup of sherry and heat through. Serve with white rice, black beans and garnish with bananas sautéed in butter.

> **To serve without freezing, stir in sherry and heat through.*

NOTES ABOUT MEAT

Slices of roast meat can be wrapped in foil, placed in a container and frozen for about 3 weeks. Meat packed in gravy keeps longer.

Spaghetti meat sauce freezes well as do all stews, undercooked. Potatoes or pastas should not be added before freezing.

Meat balls can be frozen with or without a sauce.

poultry

6

CHICKEN AND SWEETBREADS SUISSE

(4 servings)

Sweetbreads, 1 pair
Vinegar, 1 tablespoon
Roasting chicken, 4 to 4½
    pounds, cut into serving pieces
Salt, pepper and garlic powder
Butter, 12 tablespoons
Grated Swiss cheese, ½ cup
Small whole mushrooms, ½ cup

Flour, 2 tablespoons
Chicken broth, 1¾ cups
Dry Port wine or Madeira,
    ½ cup
Bread crumbs, ½ cup
Grated Parmesan cheese,
    2 tablespoons

1. Soak sweetbreads in cold water for 15 minutes. Drain. Place in boiling water to cover. Add vinegar and simmer for 20 minutes. Drain and cool in ice water for 10 minutes. Remove all membranes, tissue and fat. Slice diagonally.

2. Sprinkle chicken with salt, pepper and garlic powder. Heat 4 tablespoons of butter in heavy skillet and sauté chicken slowly till golden. Cover and simmer for 15 minutes. Remove to casserole. Sprinkle with ¼ cup of Swiss cheese.

3. Add 4 tablespoons of butter to same skillet. Sauté sweetbreads and mushrooms for 4 minutes. Drain, reserving liquid and add to casserole. Sprinkle with remaining ¼ cup of Swiss cheese.

4. Melt 2 tablespoons of butter in skillet. Blend in flour. Gradually add broth and stir until thickened. Add sweetbread-mushroom liquid and wine. Pour sauce over casserole. Sprinkle with bread crumbs, Parmesan cheese, and dots of remaining butter.* Cool. Wrap. Freeze.

slice
sweetbreads
diagonally

Serving day: Bake, uncovered, at 350° F. for 2 hours.

> *To serve without freezing, bake, uncovered, for 1½ hours.

POULET A LA VALLEE D'AUGE

(*4 servings*)

Roasting chicken, 4 to 4½ pounds
Salt, pepper, and garlic powder
Butter, 6 tablespoons
Brandy or sherry, ⅓ cup
Onion, chopped, 1
Celery, chopped, 1 stalk

Tart, firm apples, 4
Flour, 3 tablespoons
Chicken broth, 1½ cups
Salt, 1½ teaspoons
Pepper, ⅛ teaspoon
Tarragon, ½ teaspoon
Heavy cream, ½ cup

1. Cut chicken into serving pieces. Sprinkle with salt, pepper, and garlic powder. Heat 3 tablespoons of butter in heavy skillet and brown chicken in it over moderate heat. Heat brandy in a small pan and pour over chicken. Remove chicken.

2. Add 2 tablespoons of butter to same pan. Add onion, celery, and 2 apples, peeled and sliced thin. Cover and cook for 15 minutes. Stir in flour. Gradually add broth and cook over low heat, stirring until thickened. Add seasonings.

3. Put back chicken. Cover and simmer for 30 minutes. Cool. Pour chicken and sauce into casserole.* Wrap and freeze.

Serving day: Heat covered casserole at 350° F. for 1½ hours. Twenty minutes before chicken is finished, whip the cream and fold into sauce. Core 2 apples and slice into thick rings. Place on top of casserole and bake uncovered for remaining time.

> *To serve without freezing, heat covered casserole at 350° F. for 1 hour, adding cream and apples as directed.

slice apples into rings

CHICKEN PAPRIKA

(4 servings)

Roasting chicken, 4 to 4½
  pounds
Salt, pepper and garlic powder
Butter, 5 tablespoons
Onion, sliced, 1
Carrot, sliced, 1
Celery, sliced, 1 stalk
Paprika, 2 tablespoons

Flour, 3 tablespoons
Tomato paste, 1 tablespoon
Salt, ½ teaspoon
Pepper, ⅛ teaspoon
Chicken broth, 1¾ cups
Sour cream, ½ cup
Parmesan cheese, grated,
  3 tablespoons

1. Cut chicken into serving pieces. Sprinkle with salt, pepper, and garlic powder. Heat 3 tablespoons butter in heavy saucepan and brown chicken slowly in it. Remove chicken.

2. Add 1 tablespoon butter to same pan. Add onion, carrot, and celery, and cook slowly for 5 or 10 minutes. Add paprika and cook another 3 minutes. Stir in flour, tomato paste, salt and pepper. Gradually add broth and cook over low heat, stirring until thickened and boiling. Simmer for 15 minutes.

3. Put back chicken and simmer for 30 minutes. Remove chicken to casserole. Add sour cream and 1 tablespoon grated cheese to sauce and spoon it over chicken.* Cool, wrap and freeze.

Serving day: Heat covered casserole in 350° F. oven for 1½ hours. Before serving, sprinkle with 2 tablespoons grated cheese and 1 tablespoon butter. Brown under broiler.

> *To serve without freezing, heat covered casserole at 350° F. for 45 minutes. Sprinkle with cheese and butter and brown under broiler.*

CHICKEN TARRAGON WITH MUSHROOMS

(4 servings)

Roasting chicken, 4 to 4½
  pounds
Salt, pepper, garlic powder
Butter, 4 tablespoons

Mushrooms, sliced caps, ½ cup
  (4 oz. can, drained)
Tarragon, 3 tablespoons
Dry white wine, ¾ cup

1. Cut chicken into serving pieces. Sprinkle with salt, pepper and garlic powder. Heat 3 tablespoons butter in heavy saucepan. Brown chicken slowly in it. Remove.

2. Add 1 tablespoon butter to pan. Sauté mushrooms for 4 minutes. Remove.

3. Put back chicken and sprinkle with tarragon, turning until well covered. Add wine and mushrooms. Cover and simmer for 30 minutes.* Remove to casserole. Cool, wrap and freeze.

Serving day: Heat covered casserole at 350° F. for 1½ hours.

To serve without freezing, simmer for 45 minutes to 1 hour longer.

COQ AU VIN
(4 servings)

Salt pork, diced, ⅛ pound
Small white onions, peeled, 12
Small whole mushroom caps,
  ½ pound
Roasting chicken, 4 to 4½
  pounds, cut into serving pieces
Salt, pepper and garlic powder
Flour
Butter, 3 tablespoons

Oil, 3 tablespoons
Brandy, ¼ cup
Garlic, crushed, 2 cloves
Parsley, minced, 1 teaspoon
Tarragon, ½ teaspoon
Thyme, ¼ teaspoon
Bay leaf, 1
Dry red wine, 1½ cups

1. In a heavy skillet, slowly cook pork until bits are golden brown. Remove them with a slotted spoon and drain on paper towels. Add onions to pan and brown lightly. Remove from pan. Sauté mushrooms for 1 minute. Remove.

2. Sprinkle chicken with salt, pepper and garlic powder. Dredge lightly in flour. Pour off fat in pan and add butter and oil. Heat and brown chicken on all sides.

3. Heat brandy in a small pan, ignite and pour over chicken in skillet. Sprinkle chicken with crushed garlic, herbs and seasonings. Add browned pork bits, onions and half the mushrooms. Pour in wine. Cover and simmer for 30 minutes. Remove to casserole.* Cool, wrap and freeze. Place the reserved mushrooms in small freezer container and freeze.

Serving day: Bake covered casserole at 350° F. for 1½ hours. Thirty minutes before serving, place reserved mushrooms on top of casserole and finish heating.

> *To serve without freezing, bake covered casserole in 350° F. oven for 1 hour, adding reserved mushrooms 10 minutes before serving.*

CHICKEN-KUMQUAT
(4 to 5 servings)

Roasting chicken, 4 to 4½ pounds, cut into serving pieces
Curry, 1 teaspoon
Ground ginger, 1 teaspoon
Thyme, ½ teaspoon
Orégano, ½ teaspoon
Pepper, ⅛ teaspoon
Garlic, crushed, 3 cloves
Onion, chopped, 2
Soy sauce, ¼ cup

Lime juice, ¼ cup
Dry white wine, 1 cup
Butter, 2 tablespoons
Oil, 1 tablespoon
Preserved kumquats, sliced, ⅔ cup (9-oz.)
Shredded coconut, ¼ cup
Fresh pineapple, diced, ½ cup (or canned chunks)

1. Place chicken in large bowl. Sprinkle with herbs, garlic and onion, turning chicken until well-coated. Add soy sauce, lime juice, and ½ cup wine. Cover bowl and place in refrigerator for 5 hours or overnight, turning chicken occasionally in marinade.

2. Remove chicken and let drain, reserving marinade. Pat dry. Heat butter and oil in skillet and brown chicken on all sides.

3. Remove chicken. Add remaining ½ cup wine to pan and scrape up browned bits. Put back chicken and add reserved marinade. Cover and simmer for 45 minutes. Cool. Place in casserole,* wrap and freeze.

Serving day: Bake covered casserole in 350° F. oven for 45 minutes. Add kumquats, coconut and pineapple and bake, uncovered, for 30 minutes. Serve with rice.

> *To serve without freezing, bake covered casserole in 350° oven for 15 minutes. Add fruit and bake, uncovered, for 30 minutes.*

slice kumquats

SUPREME DE VOLAILLE VERONIQUE
Boneless Chicken Breasts with Grapes

(12 servings)

Half chicken breasts, boned and
  skinned, 12
Salt and pepper
Garlic, crushed, 4 cloves
Flour
Butter, 4 tablespoons
Oil, 3 tablespoons
Dry sherry, ½ cup
Onion, finely minced, 2
Mushrooms, sliced, ¾ pound

Flour, 2 tablespoons
Chicken broth, 2 cups
Dry white wine, ½ cup
Salt, ½ teaspoon
Pepper, ⅛ teaspoon
Cooked ham, shredded, 1 cup
Seedless white grapes, 1 cup
  (½ of 1 lb. 2 oz. can)
Hollandaise Sauce, 2 cups
  (see index)

1. Sprinkle both sides of chicken with salt and pepper and spread with crushed garlic. Dredge lightly with flour. Heat 3 tablespoons of butter and oil in heavy skillet and sauté chicken until golden brown. Remove chicken to shallow casserole. Heat sherry and pour over chicken.

2. Add to skillet, 1 tablespoon of butter and sauté onions until soft and transparent. Add mushrooms and cook for 2 minutes. Blend in flour. Gradually add broth and cook, stirring until smooth. Add wine, seasoning and ham. Pour sauce over chicken in casserole.* Cool. Wrap in foil. Freeze.

Serving day: Transfer casserole to room temperature 1 or 2 hours before heating. Bake casserole, covered, at 350° F. for 1 to 1½ hours. Uncover and stir grapes into sauce. Spoon reheated Hollandaise Sauce over the chicken and brown briefly under the broiler.

*To serve without freezing, bake covered casserole in 350° oven for 45 minutes. Finish as directed.

PETTI DI POLLO LOMBARDY
Boneless Chicken Breasts, Italian Style

(12 servings)

Half chicken breasts, boned, 12
Salt and pepper
Garlic, crushed, 4 cloves
Flour
Butter, 3 tablespoons
Oil, 3 tablespoons

Dried tarragon, ½ teaspoon
Chicken broth, 1½ cups
Dry white wine, ½ cup
Boiled ham, 12 slices
Mozzarella cheese, 12 thin slices

1. Sprinkle both sides of chicken with salt and pepper and spread with crushed garlic. Dredge lightly with flour. Heat butter and oil in heavy skillet and sauté chicken until golden brown.

2. Remove chicken to shallow casserole and sprinkle with tarragon. Add broth to skillet and heat while scraping up the brown particles. Add wine, bring to a boil and pour over chicken.* Cool. Cover casserole with foil and freeze.

Serving day: Transfer casserole to room temperature 1 or 2 hours before heating. Bake casserole, covered, in 350° F. oven for 1 hour. Uncover and top each breast half with 1 slice of ham. Cover and bake an additional 20 minutes. About 5 minutes before serving, top ham with 1 slice of mozzarella. Bake uncovered for about 5 minutes, until cheese is melted.

top each breast
with ham

Note: Have the butcher bone and split the whole breasts. It is not necessary to remove the skin.

> *To serve without freezing, bake covered casserole at 350° F. for 30 minutes. Finish as directed.*

CHICKEN AND OYSTER PIE

(8 individual pies)

PASTRY

Flour, 2 cups
Salt, 1 teaspoon

Butter, ¾ cup (1½ sticks)
Ice water, ¼ cup

FILLING

Half chicken breasts, skinned
   and boned, 12
Salt, pepper, and garlic powder
Butter, ¼ pound
Shallots or scallions, chopped,
   3 tablespoons
Sherry, 1 cup
Thyme, 1 teaspoon
Garlic, crushed, 4 cloves

Flour, 3 tablespoons
Light cream, 1 cup
Fresh oysters, 1½ pints
Salt, ½ teaspoon
White pepper, ⅛ teaspoon
Paprika, ¼ teaspoon
Water chestnuts, sliced, 2 cans,
   5-oz. each (1½ cups)
Mushrooms, 16 large

*put into well
salt, butter and
ice water*

1. Put flour in a large bowl, making a well in the center. Put into well, salt, butter and ice water. Work together with fingers into a smooth paste. Gradually work in the flour with fingers and knead lightly. Form into a ball, wrap in wax paper and chill for 30 minutes or longer.

*work with
fingers into
a paste*

2. Sprinkle chicken with salt, pepper and garlic powder. Heat 4 tablespoons butter in a heavy skillet and sauté chicken until golden brown. Remove. Add shallots to pan and cook over moderate heat until wilted (about 3 minutes). Add sherry and bring to a boil, scraping up the browned bits in the pan. Put back chicken and sprinkle with thyme, cover and simmer for 30 minutes.

3. Heat 3 tablespoons of butter in a skillet and sauté garlic over low heat for 1 minute. Blend in flour. Gradually add cream, stirring constantly until thick and smooth. Drain oysters and add liquid to the sauce. Bring to a boil. Add seasoning, water chestnuts and oysters and cook for 2 minutes.

4. Remove stems from mushrooms. Brush caps with 1 tablespoon melted butter. Put under hot broiler, cap side up and broil for 2 minutes.

5. Place chicken with cooking liquid in 8 individual casseroles (about 5 inches in diameter). Allow 1½ breasts per portion. Pour on oyster-cream sauce, distributing oysters equally. Top each casserole with 2 mushroom caps, rounded side up. Refrigerate casseroles.

*top casserole with
mushroom caps,
rounded side up*

6. Divide pastry into 8 parts. Roll out each part in a circle a little wider than top of casserole. Beat an egg with a little water and brush on casserole rims. Place pastry on top and press to seal. Brush top with beaten egg.* Wrap and freeze.

Serving day: Prick crusts with a fork to let steam escape. Bake in 375° F. oven for 1 hour, until golden brown and bubbly. Serve with a green salad mixed with zucchini and artichoke hearts à la grecque. If necessary, pies can wait another 30 minutes in a 250° F. oven.

> **To serve without freezing, refrigerate for 30 minutes. Prick and bake in 375° F. oven for 45 minutes.*

seal edges
with fork

STUFFED CHICKEN BREASTS IN PASTRY CRUST
(serves 8)

PASTRY

Flour, 2 cups	Butter, ¾ cup (1½ sticks)
Salt, 1 teaspoon	Ice water, ¼ cup

CHICKEN

Chicken fat, 4 tablespoons	Salt, 2 teaspoons
Garlic, crushed, 2 cloves	Sherry, 1 cup
Onions, chopped, 2 large	Small whole chicken breasts,
Chicken livers, 6	boned and skinned, 8
Mushrooms, coarsely chopped, ½ pound	Salt, pepper and garlic powder
Almonds, ground, ½ cup	Butter, 4 tablespoons
Parsley, minced, 2 tablespoons	Potato flour, 1 tablespoon
	Chicken broth, 2 cups

PASTRY

1. Put flour in a large bowl. Make a well in the center and put in the salt, butter and ice water. Using fingers, gradually work center ingredients to a smooth paste. Gradually work in the flour, kneading lightly. Form into a ball, wrap in wax paper and chill for 30 minutes or more.

open breasts
and pound
to flatten

CHICKEN

2. Melt chicken fat in skillet. Sauté garlic and onions until wilted. Add livers and sauté on all sides until browned but not dry (about 3 or 4 minutes). Add mushrooms to pan and cook for 3 minutes. Remove sautéed ingredients with the pan juices to chopping bowl and chop. Mix in almonds, parsley, salt and 2 tablespoons of sherry.

3. Spread open chicken breasts (like butterfly, attached at the middle). Place between 2 sheets of wax paper and pound with a wooden mallet or flat side of heavy knife until somewhat flattened out. Sprinkle with salt, pepper and garlic powder. Place a portion of stuffing on one half of each chicken breast. Fold the other half breast over the stuffing. Fold up the bottom edges like an envelope to enclose the stuffing. Secure with toothpicks.

4. Heat butter in skillet and brown chicken very quickly on all sides. Transfer chicken to shallow casserole. Add remaining sherry to skillet and heat, stirring up the browned bits. Pour over chicken in the casserole. Bake covered, at 350° F. for 35 minutes. Remove chicken from casserole, remove toothpicks and chill in refrigerator.

5. Blend potato flour into juices remaining in roasting pan. Add broth and cook, stirring, until thickened and smooth. Cool. Pour into container and freeze.

6. Divide dough into 8 parts. Roll each part into a rectangle, large enough to enclose 1 breast. Place chilled chicken on one-half of rectangle and fold the other half over. Fold up ends to completely enclose the chicken. Beat egg with a little water and brush on pastry.* Wrap in foil and freeze.

Serving day: Bake on greased cooky sheet in a 400° F. oven for 50 minutes, until golden brown. Serve with Zucchini Mousse or creamed spinach garnished with toasted slivered almonds and a salad of cooked lentils and chopped scallions marinated in French dressing.

*To serve without freezing, bake at 400° F for 35 minutes. Do not freeze gravy.

place
stuffing
on chicken

fold over
secure with
toothpicks

cooled chicken
on pastry

fold over
and fold
up ends

CHICKEN CREPES
(14 to 16)

BATTER

Eggs, 2
Milk, 1 cup
Butter, melted and cooled,
  2 tablespoons

Salt, ½ teaspoon
Cayenne, dash
Nutmeg, ⅛ teaspoon
Flour, sifted, ½ cup

FILLING

Butter, 4 tablespoons
Onions, chopped, 2
Mushrooms, thinly sliced,
  2 cups (½ pound)
Cooked spinach, drained and
  chopped, ¼ cup (½ of 10-oz.
  frozen package)

Cooked chicken, coarsely
  chopped, 2 cups
Sour cream, 4 tablespoons
Sherry, 2 tablespoons
Salt, ½ teaspoon
Cayenne, dash

SAUCE

Butter, 4 tablespoons
Flour, 4 tablespoons
Chicken broth, 2 cups
Milk, 1 cup
Parmesan cheese, grated, ½ cup

Swiss cheese or Gruyère, grated
  ½ cup
Salt to taste
Cayenne, dash
Saffron, ⅛ teaspoon (optional)
Sherry, ½ cup

BATTER

1. Beat eggs with milk, butter and seasoning. Gradually add flour, beating until smooth. Refrigerate, covered, for 2 hours or more.

FILLING

2. Heat butter in large skillet. Sauté onions until soft and golden. Add mushrooms and cook for 4 minutes, stirring occasionally. Stir in spinach, chicken, sour cream, sherry, salt and cayenne. Remove from heat and refrigerate until needed.

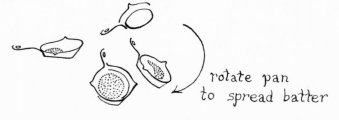

rotate pan
to spread batter

CREPES

3. Heat a 6″ skillet and grease lightly. Pour in about 2 table-spoons of batter, rotating pan quickly to spread batter evenly over bottom. Cook over brisk heat until bubbly and lightly browned on one side. Turn and brown the other side lightly. Remove to wax paper. Repeat process until batter is used.

4. Place 2 tablespoons of filling in center of each crêpe. Flap one side of crêpe over filling. Fold ends in and roll up.* Place seam side down on flat surface and chill in freezer for 1 hour. Pack in a container with freezer paper between layers and freeze.

SAUCE

Melt butter. Blend in flour until smooth. Gradually stir in broth and milk. Cook over low heat, stirring constantly until smooth. Add grated cheese and seasoning. Stir over low heat until cheese is melted. Remove from heat and add sherry. Cool. Pack in container and freeze.

Serving day: Thaw crêpes at room temperature for 1 hour or more. Heat sauce in a saucepan over very low heat, stirring frequently. Place crêpes on a greased, shallow baking dish, seam side down. Place 1 tablespoonful of sauce on top of each crêpe. Bake at 375° F. for 25 minutes until lightly browned. Pour on more sauce and bake another 20 to 25 minutes. Serve with remaining hot sauce.

Alternate preparation on Serving day: Thaw crêpes at room temperature for 1 hour or more. Place on greased broiler pan. Top with one tablespoon of heated sauce. Broil 3 or 4″ from heat for about 15 minutes, until nicely browned. Serve with remaining hot sauce.

> *To serve without freezing, bake as directed, reducing time to 20 minutes and 10 minutes or broil for about 10 to 12 minutes.

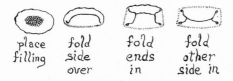

place filling   fold side over   fold ends in   fold other side in

PAELLA
(6 or 8 servings)

Orégano, 1 teaspoon
Garlic, crushed, 2 cloves
Salt, 1½ teaspoons
Pepper, ⅛ teaspoon
Olive or peanut oil, 4 tablespoons
Vinegar, 1 teaspoon
Roasting chicken, 4 pounds, cut into small serving pieces
Butter, 4 tablespoons
Onion, chopped, 1
Pepperoni sausage, chopped, 1
Raw rice, 2 cups

Cooked ham, diced, ½ pound
Zucchini, unpeeled, thickly sliced, 2 cups
Cooked lobster, diced, 1 cup
Raw shrimp, shelled and cleaned, 1 pound
Whole tomatoes, with liquid, 1 lb. can
Chicken broth, 4 cups
Saffron, 1 teaspoon
Mussels, 1 quart

saffron

1. Combine orégano, half the garlic, salt, pepper, 2 tablespoons oil, and vinegar. Rub thoroughly into chicken. Heat remaining oil and 2 tablespoons of butter in heavy skillet. Brown chicken over moderate heat. Remove.

2. Add 1 tablespoon of butter to skillet and sauté onion, remaining garlic, and pepperoni slices. Add 1 tablespoon of butter and sauté rice until golden, about 4 minutes. Stir in ham, zucchini, lobster, shrimp and chicken. Cook for 5 or 10 minutes over moderate heat. Add tomatoes and 2 cups of broth. Bring to a boil.

3. Transfer to a large casserole. Cover and bake in 375° F. oven for 30 minutes.* Cool quickly. Wrap and freeze.

Serving day: Add 1 cup of broth, cover and bake at 375° F. for 45 minutes. Dissolve saffron in 1 cup of broth. Stir into casserole, cover and bake for 45 minutes or more. When ready to serve, steam mussels until shells open, and place on top of casserole. Serve with tossed green salad and garlic bread.

place mussels on top of casserole

*To serve without freezing, add saffron, dissolved in 2 cups of broth and bake, uncovered, in 375° F. oven for 1 hour or more. Finish as directed.

TURKEY AMANDINE
(14 to 16 servings — 1¼ gallons)

Butter or margarine, ¾ pound
Onions, finely chopped, 6
Mushrooms, sliced in half,
   1 pound
Flour, 1¼ cups
Salt, 1 teaspoon
Pepper, ¼ teaspoon
Curry powder, 1½ teaspoons
Dry mustard, 1½ teaspoons
Cayenne, dash

Chicken broth, 6 cups
Light cream, 2 cups
Almonds, blanched, sliced and
   toasted, 2 cups (2 cans,
   6-oz. each)
Cooked turkey, cut up, 3 quarts
   (10-pound turkey)
Sherry, 1 cup
Chopped parsley

1. Melt 6 tablespoons butter in Dutch oven. Sauté onions till golden. Add mushrooms and sauté for 4 minutes. Remove onions and mushrooms.

2. Melt remaining butter. Blend in flour and seasonings. Add broth. Cook over low heat, stirring frequently, until smooth and thick. Stir in cream. Add turkey, almonds, sautéed onions and mushrooms and mix thoroughly.* Cool. Pour into containers. (If gallon container is used, fill half way, then place a double thickness of freezer paper on surface, and fill remaining half.) Freeze.

Serving day: Heat in double boiler for 1 hour or more until thoroughly hot. Before serving, add sherry and reheat. Sprinkle with chopped parsley and serve with Chinese noodles, rice, or hot cream puffs.

     *To serve without freezing, heat thoroughly and
     add sherry.

CHICKEN SALAD

Fowl, 5 pounds, 1
Carrot, sliced, 1
Onion, quartered, 1
Celery, including leaves, 1 stalk

Parsley, 4 sprigs
Dill, 4 sprigs
Salt, 1 tablespoon
Peppercorns, 4

fill container half-
way — place foil or
paper on surface

1. Place chicken in a large kettle with cold water to barely cover. Bring to a boil and remove scum. Add carrot, onion, celery,

parsley, dill, salt and peppercorns. Cover and simmer for about 2 hours until chicken in tender. Cool the chicken in the broth.

2. When cool, take out chicken. Discard skin* and cut meat from bones in the largest pieces you can. Wrap chicken in 4 separate foil packages and pack in plastic bag or container. Freeze. Yields 4 cups.

Serving day:

Celery, chopped, 1 stalk
Raw mushrooms, sliced, ½ cup
Salad oil, 6 tablespoons
Lemon juice, 2 tablespoons
Garlic, crushed, 1 clove
Dill seed, 2 teaspoons

Salt, ¾ teaspoon
Pepper, ¼ teaspoon
Mayonnaise, ½ cup
Almonds, slivered and toasted, ½ cup

Defrost chicken at room temperature for about 1 hour. Dice it and mix with celery, mushrooms, oil, lemon juice, garlic, dill seed, salt and pepper. Refrigerate for 1 hour or more. When ready to serve, mix with mayonnaise and almonds. Arrange on lettuce leaves, garnished with black olives and marinated artichoke hearts.

*To serve without freezing, dice chicken and proceed as directed.

GLAZED ROAST DUCK WITH WALNUTS
(6 to 8 servings)

Ducks, 4 to 5 pounds each, 2
Salt, pepper, and garlic powder
Onions, 2
Oranges, quartered, 2

Currant jelly, ½ cup
Orange juice, ½ cup
Red wine, ½ cup
Chopped walnuts, 1 cup

Cut under duck skin, separating it from fat to allow the fat to drain out. Sprinkle inside and out with salt, pepper, and garlic powder. Place onion and quartered orange in each cavity. Roast on a rack, uncovered, at 325° F. for 2 hours, pouring off fat occasionally. Cool and cut in quarters.* Wrap in foil and freeze.

cut under duck skin

Night before serving: Place duck in refrigerator to thaw for 24 hours.

Serving day: Remove to room temperature 1 hour before reheating. Heat together jelly, orange juice and wine. Stir until thick and smooth. Stir in nuts. Brush ducks liberally with sauce. Brown at 350° F. for 1 hour, basting occasionally. Serve with wild rice.

> **To serve without freezing, make the sauce. Finish as directed.*

BRAISED DUCK WITH CHERRIES

(4 servings)

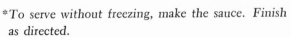

Duck, quartered, 6 pound	Tarragon, ⅛ teaspoon
Onion, chopped, 1	Pitted black cherries, 1 lb. can
Garlic, crushed, 1 clove	Cornstarch, 2 tablespoons
Red wine, 1 cup	Duck giblet or chicken broth,
Salt, ½ teaspoon	½ cup

1. Place duck, skin side down, in heavy skillet over moderate heat. Cook for 1 hour, until brown and crisp on both sides, pouring off fat occasionally.

2. Remove duck to casserole and drain all but 1 tablespoon fat from pan. Add onion and garlic to pan and sauté for 3 minutes. Add wine and seasonings. Pour over duck in casserole. Cover and cook in 350° F. oven for 1 hour.* Cool, wrap and freeze.

Serving day: Uncover casserole and heat in 350° F. oven for 30 to 45 minutes. Drain cherries, reserving ¾ cup of juice. Combine juice with cornstarch. Heat broth and stir in cherry juice. Cook, stirring constantly until thickened. Add cherries and pour over duck. Cover casserole and cook in 350° F. oven for 30 minutes more.

> **To serve without freezing, add cherries and finish as directed.*

drain cherries

TIPSY DUCK

(8 portions)

Duck, quartered, 2
Salt and pepper
Garlic, crushed, 4 cloves
Onions, finely chopped, 2
Parsley, minced, 2 tablespoons
Celery, finely chopped, 2 stalks
Dry red wine, 3 cups
Brandy, ¾ cup

Bay leaves, 4
Thyme, 1 teaspoon
Salt pork, ½ pound
Mushrooms, sliced, 3 cups
  (1 pound)
Chestnuts, boiled, peeled and
  chopped, 1½ cups (¾ pound
  in shell)

1. Wash duck. Remove as much fat as possible from beneath the skin. Sprinkle with salt and pepper. Place in a large bowl with garlic, onions, parsley, celery, wine, brandy, bay leaves and thyme. Cover and refrigerate overnight.

2. Remove duck and pat dry. Reserve marinade. Cook salt pork in a heavy Dutch oven until it is almost crisp. Remove pork. Add duck and brown very well on all sides. When brown, remove and drain on paper towelling. Empty all fat from pan. Put back duck with wine marinade. Cover and simmer for 1 hour. Remove duck, without sauce, to a shallow casserole. Cover and refrigerate. Chill sauce in freezer for about 30 minutes. Refrigerate sauce until fat congeals. Remove fat. Combine sauce with mushrooms and chestnuts and cook for 5 minutes. Pour over duck.* Cool. Wrap and freeze.

Serving day: Bake, covered, in 350° F. oven for 1½ hours. Uncover, and bake for 30 minutes more.

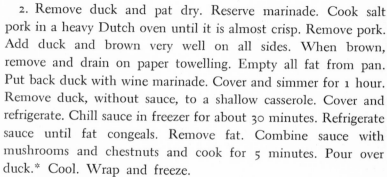

*To serve without freezing, bake covered at 350° F. for 45 minutes. Finish as directed.

EXTRA NOTES ABOUT POULTRY

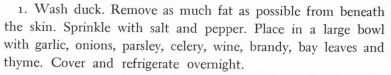

To freeze roasted chicken or turkey for later use, remove from bone in the largest pieces possible and wrap in small foil packages, placed inside a container or bag. To use, thaw and cut up for salad or heat in a sauce or grind for a mousse or aspic.

wrap in foil
packages....pack
in container

fish

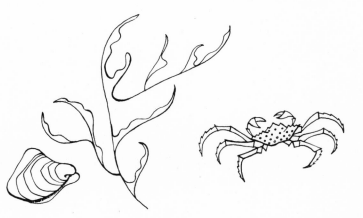

7

COULIBIAC OF SALMON AND LOBSTER
Hot or Cold
(8 individual turnovers)

PASTRY

Cream cheese, ½ pound
Salt butter, ½ pound
Heavy cream, ½ cup

Sugar, 1 teaspoon
Flour, 2½ cups

FILLING

White wine, 1 cup
Water, 2 cups
Onion, 1
Celery, 1 stalk
Garlic, crushed, 1 clove
Parsley, 3 sprigs
Dill, 3 sprigs
Bay leaf, 1
Salt, 2 teaspoons
Pepper, ⅛ teaspoon
Thyme, ½ teaspoon
Fresh or frozen salmon, in one
    piece, 1½ pounds

Water, 1 quart
Salt, 1 tablespoon
Peppercorns, 2
Vinegar, 1 tablespoon
Frozen lobster tail, ½ pound
Butter, 4 tablespoons
Shallots, chopped, ¼ cup
Raw rice, ½ cup
Mushrooms, sliced, ½ pound
Salt, 1 teaspoon
Pepper, ¼ teaspoon
Sour cream, ½ cup
Fresh dill, minced, 2 tablespoons
Egg yolk, 1

PASTRY

1. With fingers, blend cream cheese, butter, cream, and sugar to a creamy paste. Gradually add flour and work in with fingers until very well blended. Form into a ball and wrap in wax paper. Refrigerate overnight or at least 2 hours.

FILLING

2. Place in a large saucepan the wine, water, onion, celery, garlic, parsley, dill, bay leaf, 2 teaspoons salt, pepper and thyme. Bring to a boil, cover and simmer for 20 minutes. Tie up salmon in a cheesecloth bag and add to pot. Cover and simmer for 15 minutes or until almost tender. Remove salmon and let cool. Strain the liquid and reserve it.

3. Bring the quart of water to a boil with 1 tablespoon salt, peppercorns and vinegar. Add lobster tail and cook for 12 minutes. Cool and remove lobster meat.

4. Heat 2 tablespoons of butter and sauté shallots until wilted. Add rice and sauté until golden. Stir in 1¼ cups of reserved salmon liquid and bring to a boil. Transfer to a casserole and bake rice, covered, at 350° F. for 45 minutes. Cool and reserve.

5. Heat remaining 2 tablespoons of butter and sauté mushrooms for 3 minutes. Stir in salt and pepper. Remove skin and bones from salmon and flake in large pieces. Lightly mix together salmon, lobster, mushrooms with their liquid, sour cream and dill.

6. Cut chilled dough into 8 parts. Roll out each part into a circle, less than ¼" thick. Place a layer of rice on ½ of each circle. On top of this, place the fish mixture and top with another layer of rice. Fold the other half of pastry over the filling to form a semi-circular turnover. Moisten edges with water and fold the bottom edge up over the top, firmly pressing together with the fingers, to completely seal in filling. Beat egg yolk with water and brush on top.* Freeze on flat surface for 1 hour. When frozen, wrap in foil, freezer paper, or plastic bag and return to freezer.

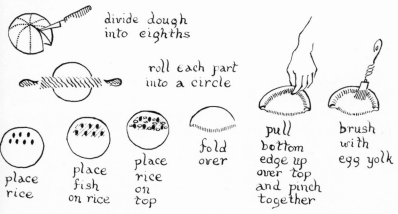

divide dough into eighths

roll each part into a circle

place rice

place fish on rice

place rice on top

fold over

pull bottom edge up over top and pinch together

brush with egg yolk

Serving day: Cut a slit in top of pastry and bake in 425° F. oven for 20 minutes. Reduce heat to 400° F. and bake for another 25 minutes until golden brown, hot and bubbly. Serve with hot butter sauce (recipe follows). To serve cold, cool and chill in refrigerator. Serve with sour cream, mixed with chopped chives, dill and parsley. For dinner, serve preceded by fresh Pea Soup. Also makes an excellent luncheon or late supper dish, served with a salad of marinated asparagus tips.

Note: Two cups of canned salmon, 1 cup of canned lobster and 1 can of 3-oz. sliced mushrooms may be substituted for the fresh ingredients. (It won't be as good.) When cooking the rice, use ¾ cup of water and ½ cup clam juice rather than the salmon poaching liquid.

> **To serve without freezing, cut a slit in pastry top. Bake in 425° F. oven for about 25 minutes until golden brown.*

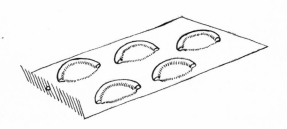

B U T T E R   S A U C E

Butter, 6 tablespoons
Flour, 3 tablespoons
Salt, ½ teaspoon
White pepper, ⅛ teaspoon

Fish stock, 1½ cups (or ¾ cup
  clam juice and ¾ cup water)
Lemon juice, 1 teaspoon

Melt 3 tablespoons of butter. Blend in flour and seasoning. Heat fish stock and gradually add, stirring constantly until smooth. Boil for 4 or 5 minutes. Stir in lemon juice. Add remaining butter, a tablespoon at a time. Serve immediately while butter is still foamy.

QUENELLES de POISSON aux SAUCE CARDINAL
Fish Dumplings with Lobster Sauce

(about 40 quenelles)

Water, 1 cup
Salt, 1¼ teaspoons
Butter, 10 tablespoons
Sifted flour, 1 cup
Eggs, 6

Halibut or haddock, ground,
  1½ pounds
White pepper, ¼ teaspoon
Nutmeg, ¼ teaspoon

1. Heat water and salt in saucepan until boiling. Add 4 tablespoons of butter and slowly melt. Remove from heat and add flour all at once, stirring with a wooden spoon to blend thoroughly. Put back over moderate heat and beat vigorously until mixture leaves the side of the pan and forms a smooth, shiny ball. Transfer to mixing bowl.

2. Add 4 eggs, one at a time, beating thoroughly after each addition. Add fish, pepper and nutmeg and beat for 6 minutes at high speed. Cream remaining 6 tablespoons of butter with a wooden spoon and gradually beat into mixture. Beat in remaining 2 eggs, one at a time. Spread mixture on flat pan, and chill in a freezer for 15 minutes (not directly on freezing coils), or in refrigerator for 6 hours or overnight.

3. To form mixture into small sausage-shaped quenelles, take it by rounded tablespoons and lightly roll by hand on a floured board. In a large roasting pan, bring to a boil 4" of fish stock or salted water. Reduce heat to a simmer and carefully slip in quenelles. Poach, uncovered, for 20 minutes. Gently turn over and poach 5 minutes longer. Remove carefully with a slotted spoon and drain on a towel.* When cool and firm, carefully place on a flat surface and place in freezer. When frozen, pack in a container. Return to freezer.

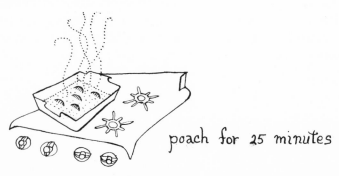

poach for 25 minutes

Serving day: Place frozen quenelles on a greased baking and serving dish or in individual greased scallop shells. Heat in 350° F. oven for 20 to 25 minutes. Heat Sauce Cardinal in a double boiler or over direct low heat, and pour over heated quenelles. Heat frozen lobster meat in a little butter and garnish dish. Serve very hot. Serve as a luncheon dish with a green salad garnished with marinated string beans, or as part of a buffet supper with cold sliced meats and salads. Can also be served as a hot hors d'oeuvre, or as a late supper dish with cold ratatouille.

> *To serve without freezing, place hot quenelles on a heated platter. Pour on hot sauce and garnish with lobster, sautéed in butter.

SAUCE CARDINAL
Lobster Sauce

(2 cups)

Lobster, cut in quarters, 1 pound
Oil, 4 tablespoons
Carrot, grated, 1
Onion, finely chopped, 1
Garlic, crushed, 1 clove
Parsley, minced, 1 tablespoon
Salt, ½ teaspoon
Pepper, ⅛ teaspoon

Thyme, ¼ teaspoon
Curry, ⅛ teaspoon
Bay leaf, 1
Saffron, pinch
Tomato paste, 1 tablespoon
Dry white wine, 2 cups
Water, ¾ cup
Butter, ¼ pound

1. Sauté lobster in very hot oil, tossing frequently, until shells are red (about 8 minutes). Add remaining ingredients, except water and butter, and cook over moderate heat for 10 minutes. Remove lobster and cook sauce for about 10 more minutes, until thickened. Remove bay leaf and purée sauce in blender until thickened. Refrigerate. Remove lobster meat from shells and dice. Place in container and freeze.

Make Lobster Butter.

2. Chop empty shells coarsely and put in blender with ½ cup water. Blend at high speed. Pour into double boiler with ¼ pound of butter and simmer for 15 minutes. Strain through cheesecloth into a bowl, pressing to extract butter and liquid. Return shell debris to double boiler. Add ¼ cup water and simmer for 5 minutes. Press through cheesecloth into bowl containing first extraction. Chill bowl until butter hardens on top. Skim off butter. (Yields ½ cup lobster butter.)

3. Add 4 tablespoons of lobster butter to reserved lobster sauce, beating slightly to blend. Pack in container and freeze. Pack remaining lobster butter in container and freeze. Use as sauce enrichment in any other fish dish. Add liquid remaining from butter extraction to fish stock used for poaching Quenelles. Freeze. Use as a base for another fish sauce or soup.

strain through
cheesecloth

LOBSTER AMERICAINE

(6 to 12 servings)

Lobster, cooked or canned, 2 cups
Butter, 4 tablespoons
Onion, finely chopped, 1
Garlic, crushed, 1 clove
Flour, ¼ cup
Chicken broth, 2 cups
Tomato paste, ⅓ cup

White wine, ⅓ cup
Parsley, minced, 1 tablespoon
Salt, ½ teaspoon
Pepper, ⅛ teaspoon
Cayenne, ¼ teaspoon
Cheese, grated, 1 cup
Paprika, dash

1. Drain and pick over lobster.

2. Heat butter in large skillet. Add onions and garlic. Cook for 5 minutes. Blend in flour. Gradually add broth and cook over low heat, stirring until thickened. Add tomato paste, wine, parsley, lobster, salt, pepper and cayenne.

3. Turn into 12 scallop shells, or a 1½ quart casserole. Top with grated cheese and paprika.* Cool, wrap, and freeze.

Serving day: Unwrap shells and bake in 400° F. oven. Bake shells for ½ hour, casserole for 1 hour. Serve for luncheon, late supper or as an hors d'oeuvre.

> *To serve without freezing, bake shells for 15 minutes, casseroles for 30 minutes.*

TURBAN OF SOLE
Ring Mold of Sole, stuffed with Salmon Mousse
(serves 8)

Fillets of sole (or flounder), 6
Lemon juice, 6 tablespoons
　(2 lemons)
Salt, pepper and ground dill
Fish stock or water, ½ cup
Salt, ½ teaspoon
Butter, 5 tablespoons

Flour, ½ cup
Eggs, 3
Ground salmon, ¾ pound
　(1¼ cups)
White pepper, ⅛ teaspoon
Dill weed, 2 teaspoons

1. Place fillets in a bowl with lemon juice and cold water to cover. Soak for 10 minutes. Drain and dry well. Sprinkle with salt, pepper and dill. Grease liberally a 1½ quart ring mold. Line it with the fillets, placing the white side next to the mold and the tips hanging over the sides.

2. Heat fish stock and salt until boiling. Add 2 tablespoons of butter and slowly melt. Remove from heat and add flour all at once, stirring with a wooden spoon to blend thoroughly. Put back over moderate heat and beat vigorously until mixture leaves the side of the pan and forms a smooth, shiny ball. Transfer to mixing bowl.

3. Add 2 eggs, one at a time, beating thoroughly after each addition. Add ground salmon, pepper and dill weed and beat for 6 minutes at high speed. Cream remaining 3 tablespoons of butter with a wooden spoon and gradually beat into mixture. Beat in remaining egg.

line ring
with fillets

fill with
mousse

fold tips of
fillets over

4. Fill lined mold with Mousse. Fold the tips of fillets over it.* Wrap and freeze.

Serving day: Unwrap frozen mold and place on a rack in a pan with boiling water coming to top of mold. Cover lightly with foil. Poach in 375° F. oven for 1 hour and 30 minutes. Remove mold from water and let stand for 10 minutes. Unmold onto hot platter. After 1 minute, tip platter carefully to drain off the watery liquid. Fill the center with Shrimp-Mushroom Sauce (recipe follows). Serve with hot asparagus, sprinkled with hard-cooked egg yolk or cold asparagus vinaigrette and toasted almond muffins.

tip platter to drain off liquid

> *To serve without freezing, bake as directed for 45 minutes.*

poach on rack in pan of boiling water

SHRIMP-MUSHROOM SAUCE
(*about 4½ cups*)

Butter, ½ cup
Raw shrimp, peeled and
  deveined, 1 pound
Garlic, crushed, 2 cloves
Salt, 1 teaspoon
Pepper, ¼ teaspoon

Paprika, 1 teaspoon
Brandy, ¼ cup
Flour, ¼ cup
Fish stock or half water, half
  clam juice, 2 cups
Heavy cream, ½ cup
Mushroom caps, ½ pound

Heat 6 tablespoons of butter and sauté shrimp and garlic for 3 minutes. Sprinkle with seasoning and brandy. Blend in flour. Add stock, stirring until smooth and thickened. Stir in cream. Cool. Pack in container and freeze. Sauté mushrooms in remaining butter for 3 or 4 minutes. Pack in container and freeze.

Serving day: Reheat sauce in double boiler or over low heat until hot but not boiling. Reheat mushrooms separately over low heat. Spoon shrimp sauce into center of mold and top with hot mushroom caps.

LOBSTER IN BECHAMEL SAUCE
(About 6 cups)

COOKED LOBSTER MEAT
(5 cups)

Frozen lobster tails or live
  lobsters, 4½ to 5 pounds
Water, 3 gallons

Salt, 6 tablespoons
Pepper, 1 teaspoon
Vinegar, 6 tablespoons

FISH STOCK
(2½ quarts)

Lobster shells
Water, 3 quarts
Dry white wine, ½ cup
Onion, coarsely chopped, 2
Leek, chopped, 1
Carrot, coarsely chopped, 2
Garlic, sliced, 2 cloves

Celery, chopped, 2 stalks
  with leaves
Parsley, 3 sprigs
Bay leaves, 2
Peppercorns, crushed, 6
Thyme, ½ teaspoon
Salt, 1½ teaspoons

BECHAMEL SAUCE
(3½ cups)

Butter, 5 tablespoons
Garlic, crushed, 1 clove
Onion, minced, 1 small
Fresh parsley, minced,
  2 tablespoons
Flour, 4 tablespoons

Milk, 2 cups
Fish stock, 2 cups
White pepper, ⅛ teaspoon
Nutmeg, ⅛ teaspoon
Paprika, ¼ teaspoon
Salt to taste
Mushrooms, sliced, ½ pound

LOBSTER

1. Place water and seasoning in a large kettle and bring to a boil. Add lobster, cover, and boil for 12 to 15 minutes. Remove with tongs and place in cold water. Remove meat, saving shells for stock. Dice lobster into small pieces.

STOCK

2. Combine all ingredients in a large kettle. Bring to a boil and simmer for 30 minutes. Strain. Reserve 2 cups for sauce. Freeze the rest for another dish.

SAUCE

3. Melt 4 tablespoons of butter in large skillet and sauté garlic, onion, and parsley until soft but not brown. Stir in flour until well-blended. Gradually add milk and stock and cook, stirring frequently, until thick and smooth. Add seasoning. In remaining tablespoon of butter, sauté mushrooms over moderately high heat for about 3 minutes. Add to sauce along with the lobster meat.* Cool. Pack in container. Freeze.

Serving day: Reheat in top of double boiler over simmering water and cook, stirring occasionally until hot. Serve in baked Puff Paste patty shells or Croustades. (See index.)

Note: After cooking the lobster and the fish stock you may, if more convenient, refrigerate them for 1 day before finishing the Béchamel Sauce. Store in separate containers.

Reheat to serve without freezing.

S H R I M P   M A R I N A R A
(8 servings)

Olive oil, 4 tablespoons	Salt, 1 teaspoon
Garlic, crushed, 2 cloves	Pepper, ½ teaspoon
Onions, sliced, 2	Orégano, 1½ teaspoons
Tomatoes, Italian style, 3 cups drained (2-lb. 3-oz. can)	Raw shrimp, shelled and deveined, 2 pounds

1. Heat oil in deep skillet. Brown garlic for 1 minute. Add onions and cook until soft. Add drained tomatoes to onions with salt and pepper. Simmer for 1 hour.

2. Add orégano and shrimp. Cook for 4 minutes.* Cool. Pour into containers and freeze.

Night before or *Serving day:* Thaw in refrigerator overnight or at room temperature for 4 hours. Heat in covered double boiler for 30 minutes or longer. Serve from chafing dish or serving casserole placed over a heating device.

To serve without freezing, cook 8 to 10 minutes longer.

SEA FOOD CREPE-PIE
(6 to 8 servings)

CREPES

Eggs, 2
Milk, 1 cup
Butter, melted and cooked,
  2 tablespoons

Salt, ½ teaspoon
Cayenne, dash
Nutmeg, ⅛ teaspoon
Flour, ½ cup

FILLING

Cooked crabmeat or lobster
  or shrimp, 1 pound (2 cups)
Butter, 3 tablespoons
Garlic, crushed, 1 clove
Shallots, chopped, ¼ cup
Water chestnuts, sliced, ½ cup
  (5-oz. can)

Sherry, ¼ cup
Salt, 1 teaspoon
Cayenne, ⅛ teaspoon
Dry mustard, ½ teaspoon
Nutmeg, freshly grated,
  ¼ teaspoon
Parsley, minced, ½ cup

SAUCE

Butter, 5 tablespoons
Flour, 4 tablespoons
Fish stock or clam juice, 2 cups
Milk, ½ cup
Grated Swiss cheese, 1 cup
Heavy cream, 1 cup
Salt, ½ teaspoon

Cayenne, ⅛ teaspoon
Saffron, ⅛ teaspoon
Sherry, 1 tablespoon
Cooked lobster, diced, 1 cup
Small mushroom caps, ½ pound
  (2 cups)

CREPE BATTER

1. Beat eggs with milk, butter and seasoning. Gradually add flour, beating until smooth. Refrigerate, covered, for 2 hours or more.

FILLING

2. Remove cartilage from crabmeat and flake, or chop lobster or shrimp. Heat butter and sauté garlic and shallots over low heat until wilted (about 2 minutes). Add water chestnuts and sea food. Cook for 2 minutes. Add wine and seasoning. Cook over moderate heat until liquid evaporates. Stir in parsley. Reserve.

SAUCE

3. Heat 4 tablespoons of butter. Blend in flour until smooth. Gradually stir in stock. Cook over low heat, stirring constantly until thick and smooth. Add milk, cheese, cream and seasoning and stir over heat until blended. Dissolve saffron in sherry and stir into sauce. Blend ¼ cup of sauce into filling. Add lobster to remaining sauce. Cool, pack in container and freeze. Sauté mushroom caps in remaining tablespoon of butter for 3 minutes. Cool. Pack in a small container and freeze.

PIE

4. Heat a 7½″ or 8″ skillet and grease lightly. Pour in about ¼ cup of batter, rotating pan quickly to spread batter evenly over bottom. Cook over brisk heat until bubbly and lightly browned on one side. Turn and brown the other side lightly. Remove to wax paper. Repeat process until all batter is used. (Yields 8 to 10 crêpes.)

5. Grease a 9 inch pie plate and place a crêpe in the center. Spread with a thin layer of sea food filling and cover with another crêpe. Repeat until all ingredients are used, ending with a crêpe on top.* Wrap in foil. Freeze.

Serving day: Thaw wrapped pie at room temperature for 1 hour. Reheat sauce over low heat. Unwrap pie and pour 1 cup of the reheated sauce over the top and sides. Bake in 350° F. oven for 1 hour. Five to ten minutes before serving, reheat frozen mushrooms over low heat and garnish top of finished pie. Cut into pie-shaped wedges and pass hot sauce separately. Serve for luncheon with a tomato aspic mold, garnished with asparagus and cucumbers vinaigrette.

*To serve without freezing, pour 1 cup of sauce over pie and bake at 350° F. for 30 minutes.

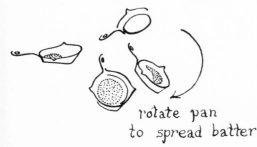

rotate pan
to spread batter

arrange crepes and sea food in layers

CRAB MEAT QUICHE
(9" pie)

PASTRY

Flour, sifted, 1 cup

Salt, ½ teaspoon

Shortening, chilled, ⅓ cup

Ice water, 2 to 3 tablespoons

FILLING

Parmesan cheese, grated, ½ cup

Crabmeat, fresh-cooked or canned, 1½ cups

Small onion, finely chopped, 1

Dry sherry, 2 tablespoons

Parsley, minced, 2 tablespoons

Salt, ½ teaspoon

Pepper, ⅛ teaspoon

Cayenne, pinch

Tarragon, ⅛ teaspoon

Eggs, 4

Cream, 2 cups

Paprika

1. Add salt to sifted flour and sift again. Cut in shortening until particles are the size of peas. Sprinkle on water, a little at a time. With a fork, press moistened particles together until dough holds together. Turn out onto wax paper and form into a ball. Chill in refrigerator for 30 minutes.

2. Roll out dough ⅛" thick into a circle 1" larger than diameter of pan. Place in pan. Trim edge about ½" above top of pan. Flute with fingers to make a standing rim. Brush with lightly beaten egg white. Place in freezer for 1 hour or more.

3. Spread grated cheese over frozen pie crust. Combine crabmeat with onion, sherry, parsley, salt, pepper, cayenne and tarragon, and spread on top of cheese. Beat eggs lightly with cream and pour over crabmeat. Sprinkle with paprika.* Freeze pie. When firm, wrap and freeze.

Serving day: Bake at 500° F. for 10 minutes. Reduce heat to 400° F. and bake for another 50 minutes, until custard is set and it is browned on top. Serve, preceded by onion soup and with a green salad for luncheon, dinner, or late supper.

*To serve without freezing, reduce final baking at 400° F. to 30 minutes.

SHRIMP AND CRAB GUMBO

(10 to 12 servings)

Bacon fat, ¼ cup
Flour, ¼ cup
Clam juice, 2 cups
Italian plum tomatoes, 3-lb. 2-oz.
  can, 4 cups
Beef broth, 1 cup
Parsley, minced, ½ cup
Bay leaf, 2
Thyme, 1 teaspoon
Tabasco, dash
Black peppercorns, 4
Crushed red pepper flakes,
  ½ teaspoon

Salt, 1 tablespoon
Cooked ham, diced, 1 slice,
  ½" thick, ½ pound
Fresh okra, whole, 1 pound
Raw shrimp, peeled and
  deveined, 2 pounds
Butter, 5 tablespoons
Garlic, crushed, 3 cloves
Onion, chopped, 2
Green peppers, cut into strips, 3
Celery, cut in ½" pieces, 4 stalks
Cooked crabmeat, 2 pounds
Filé powder, 1 tablespoon

fill container half-way... place foil or paper on surface

1. Heat bacon fat in a heavy skillet. Blend in flour, stirring occasionally, until it is dark brown. Gradually add clam juice, stirring over low heat until thick and smooth. Crush tomatoes and with their liquid add to pot. Add broth and seasoning; simmer for 20 minutes. Add to pot the ham, okra, and shrimp, simmer for 10 minutes.

2. Heat 1 tablespoon butter and sauté garlic and onions until wilted. Add remaining 4 tablespoons butter and sauté peppers and celery for 2 or 3 more minutes. Stir sautéed vegetables and crab meat into mixture.* Cool. Pour into 4 containers of 1 quart each or 2 containers of ½ gallon each with a halfway separation of 2 sheets of foil or freezer paper. Freeze.

Day before or *Serving day:* Thaw in refrigerator overnight or at room temperature for 6 hours. Reheat in double boiler over boiling water (about 45 minutes). When at the boiling point and ready to serve, remove from heat and stir in filé powder. Serve in soup bowls over a big spoonful of cooked white rice. This is good for a late supper party, followed by applesauce tarts and coffee.

Note: If fresh okra is not available, use 1 package of frozen whole okra. On the **Serving day**, add it to the thawed gumbo in the double boiler and cook, stirring gumbo as okra thaws.

*To serve without freezing, heat to boiling point.
Stir in filé powder as directed.

EXTRA NOTES ABOUT FISH

Do not freeze cooked fish except in a prepared sauce. This does not apply to shrimps, lobster or crabmeat.

When buying fish fillets, ask for head and bones and make fish stock for the freezer.

vegetables
and grains

8

BARLEY PILAF
(about 10 servings)

Butter, ¾ cup
Mushrooms, sliced, 1 pound
  about 4 cups
Onions, coarsely chopped, 4

Barley, medium, 2 cups
  (1 pound)
Rich chicken broth, 4 to 5 cups
Salt, 1 teaspoon
Pepper, ¼ teaspoon

scoop out beets

Heat 4 tablespoons of butter in skillet. Sauté mushrooms gently for 4 minutes. Remove mushrooms. Add remaining butter and cook onions till soft (about 5 minutes). Add barley, and cook until lightly browned, stirring frequently. Add mushrooms and 2 cups of broth to barley. Season. Turn into greased casserole. Cover and bake for 30 minutes at 350° F.* Remove, cool, and wrap. Freeze.

Serving day: Add 1 cup of broth to casserole, cover and bake in 350° F. oven for 1 hour. Stir in 1 more cup of broth and bake for 1 more hour. Uncover for last 30 minutes. (If necessary, this can stay in the oven longer. Add more broth, cover casserole and turn oven temperature lower.)

> *To serve without freezing, add 2 cups of broth and bake, covered, for 1½ hours; bake uncovered for 30 minutes.*

STUFFED BEETS

Large beets, 10
Salt, 2 teaspoons
Vinegar, 2 teaspoons
Cooked rice, 1 cup
Almonds, blanched and chopped,
  ½ cup

Scallions, chopped, 3 tablespoons
Fresh dill, chopped,
  2 tablespoons
Sour cream, 3 tablespoons
Salt, 1 teaspoon
Pepper, ⅛ teaspoon

1. Scrub beets. Boil in water with salt and vinegar until almost tender (about 40 minutes). Rub off skins, cut off roots and stems, and chill in refrigerator for 1 hour or more. Scoop out centers of beets with a melon ball cutter, leaving a shell about ½" thick.

2. Mix together rice, almonds, scallions, dill, sour cream and seasoning. Fill beet shells with mixture.* Wrap each beet in foil, pack in container or bag and freeze.

Serving day: Place frozen beets in pan containing a little water. Cover and bake in 375° F. oven until heated through (about 30 minutes).

> *To serve without freezing, bake as directed for 15 to 20 minutes.*

BLACK BEANS WITH RUM

Black beans, 2 cups
Cold water, 6 cups
Cooked ham, diced, ¼ pound
Garlic, crushed, 4 cloves
Onions, finely chopped, 2
Green peppers, finely chopped, 2
Salt, 2 teaspoons
Bay leaves, 2
Whole clove, 1
Thyme, ½ teaspoon
Cayenne pepper, ⅛ teaspoon
Lemon juice, 3 tablespoons
Rum, ¼ cup
Butter, 2 tablespoons

1. Soak beans in water to cover overnight, or boil 2 minutes and let soak, covered for 1 hour.

2. Drain and add 6 cups of water and all ingredients, except rum and butter. Cover and simmer for 2 hours.* Cool. Pack in freezing container or casserole. Freeze.

Serving day: Bake in covered casserole in 350° F. oven for about 45 minutes, until thoroughly hot. Stir in rum and butter and bake uncovered for 15 minutes more.

> *To serve without freezing, pour into casserole and stir in rum and butter. Bake, uncovered, at 350° F. for 15 minutes.*

BROCCOLI MOLD WITH ALMONDS
(8 servings)

Broccoli; fresh, 1 large bunch or frozen, 2 10-oz. packages
Chicken broth, ¼ cup
Butter, 3 tablespoons
Flour, 3 tablespoons
Sour cream, 1 cup
Shallots or scallions, chopped, ¼ cup
Eggs, 3

Swiss cheese, grated, ½ cup
Salt, ½ teaspoon
White pepper, ⅛ teaspoon
Whole nutmeg, grated, ½ teaspoon
Almonds, slivered and toasted, ½ cup
Green coloring, a few drops

1. Cook broccoli in salted water until barely tender and still bright green. Drain thoroughly. Discard very tough stalks and chop coarsely. (Yields about 2 cups.) Put chicken broth and chopped broccoli into blender and purée.

2. Heat butter in skillet and blend in flour. Gradually add sour cream and shallots and cook over low heat, stirring until thick and blended (about 3 or 4 minutes). Beat eggs lightly and stir into the hot sauce. Cook over low heat for 1 minute, stirring constantly. Stir in cheese until melted. Stir in seasoning, puréed broccoli, almonds, and coloring until well blended. Oil a 1 quart ringmold or 8 custard cups of 5 ounces each. Spoon in mixture.*
Cool. Wrap and freeze.

Serving day: Set ring or individual molds on a rack in pan, with boiling water extending as high as the filling. Bake in a 350° F. oven, 1½ hours for the ring, 1 hour for the individual molds. Cooking is complete when a knife inserted in the center is withdrawn, uncoated. Remove from water and allow to set for 3 or 4 minutes. To unmold, run a knife around the edges and invert onto a warm platter. Serve with sautéed mushrooms.

Note: Spinach can be used in place of broccoli. Three pounds of fresh spinach or 2 packages 10 ounces each of frozen leaf spinach.

*To serve without freezing, bake as directed—the ring for 35 minutes and the small molds for 20 minutes.

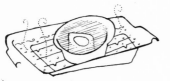

place mold on a rack in a pan of boiling water

BRAISED CHESTNUTS
(2 cups)

Chestnuts, 1 pound
Butter, 2 tablespoons
Sherry, 2 tablespoons

Potato flour, 2 teaspoons
Chicken broth, 1 cup

Cover chestnuts with boiling water and simmer for 3 minutes. Drain and remove shells and skin while hot. (Yields 2 cups.) Cut in thirds. Heat butter and sauté nuts until nicely browned on all sides. Pour on sherry. Stir flour into pan until well blended. Add broth and stir over low heat until thick and smooth. Cover and simmer for 30 minutes.* Cool. Pack in container. Freeze.

Serving day: Reheat in a covered saucepan over low heat for 30 to 40 minutes until hot. Serve, mixed with cooked, fresh or frozen string beans, broccoli, brussels sprouts, or artichoke hearts.

*Ready to serve without freezing.

CHESTNUT PUREE IN ORANGE CUPS
(6 servings)

Chestnuts, 1 pound
Chicken broth, 2 cups
Wine vinegar, 2 teaspoons
Lemon juice, 1 teaspoon
Celery, chopped, 2 stalks
Onion, chopped, 1

Melted butter, 2 tablespoons
Sour cream, ¼ cup
Salt, 1½ teaspoons
Nutmeg, pinch
Thick-skinned oranges, 3 large

1. Cover chestnuts with boiling water and simmer for 3 or 4 minutes. While hot, remove shells and skin. (Yields 2 cups.) Cook peeled chestnuts in chicken broth with vinegar, lemon juice, celery and onion until tender (about 45 minutes). Drain. Purée in blender with melted butter and sour cream. Stir in seasoning.

2. Cut oranges in half. Scoop out pulp with a grapefruit knife, being careful not to cut through skin. Ream out any remaining pulp on an orange squeezer. Cut a sawtooth edge with a scissors.

cut a saw-
tooth edge

Fill orange cups with chestnut purée.* Wrap in foil. Freeze.

Serving day: Open foil on top but leave it around orange shell. Bake at 375° F. for 45 to 50 minutes. Serve cups, arranged around a meat platter. Very good with turkey, duck or poached salmon.

*To serve without freezing, cover orange cups with foil, leaving top open. Bake 15 to 20 minutes.

EGGPLANT PARMESAN
(*4 servings*)

Whole tomatoes with liquid,
   2 cups (1 lb. can)
Water, ¼ cup and 2 tablespoons
Olive or peanut oil,
   2 tablespoons
Tomato paste, 2 tablespoons
Large eggplant, 1
Salt, pepper, and garlic powder

Eggs, 2
Bread crumbs, ½ cup
Oil, ½ cup
Garlic, minced, 2 cloves
Oregano, 1 tablespoon
Grated Parmesan cheese, ½ cup
Mozzarella cheese, sliced,
   ½ pound

1. Combine tomatoes, ¼ cup water, oil, and tomato paste in a saucepan. Simmer for 20 minutes.

2. Peel eggplant. Cut in round slices about ¼″ thick. Sprinkle with salt, pepper, and garlic powder. Beat eggs slightly with 2 tablespoons water. Dip eggplant in crumbs, then egg, and again in crumbs. Heat oil in skillet and brown garlic for 1 minute. Add eggplant and brown on both sides. Remove and drain on absorbent paper.

3. Line shallow baking dish with sauce. Place in this layers of eggplant, sauce, sprinklings of oregano, grated cheese, and mozzarella slices. Repeat the process until all ingredients are used ending with cheese.* Cover dish with foil and freeze.

slice
peeled
eggplant

Serving day: Bake, uncovered, at 350° F. for 45 minutes.

*To serve without freezing, bake for 25 minutes.

STUFFED EGGPLANT

(4 servings)

Medium eggplants, 2
Oil, 4 tablespoons
Garlic, crushed, 4 cloves
Onion, finely chopped, 1 cup
Green pepper, finely chopped, 1
Parsley, minced, 4 tablespoons
Fresh tomatoes, peeled and
  chopped, 2
Capers, washed, 1 tablespoon
Tomato paste, 1 tablespoon

Cooked rice, 1 cup
Pignole nuts, ½ cup
Dried basil, 1 teaspoon
Salt, 1 teaspoon
Black pepper, pinch
Bread crumbs, 4 tablespoons
Grated Parmesan cheese
Paprika
Butter

1. Boil eggplants whole in water to cover for 5 minutes. Drain and cool slightly. Cut in half the long way. Scoop out pulp leaving a ¾″ shell. Sprinkle shells with salt. Chop scooped-out pulp.

2. In large skillet, sauté garlic in oil for 1 minute. Add onions and green pepper and sauté until wilted. Add eggplant pulp, parsley, tomatoes, and capers and sauté for about 5 minutes. Stir in tomato paste, rice, nuts, basil, salt and pepper and mix well.

3. Fill eggplant shells with mixture. Sprinkle tops with crumbs, grated cheese and paprika.* Cool. Place filled shells on flat tray. Freeze till solid. Wrap each separately in foil or freezer paper. Return to freezer.

Serving day: Place eggplant in a shallow baking dish with about ½″ water in the bottom. Bake at 350° F. for 30 minutes. Dot tops with butter and bake at 400° F. for 10 or 15 minutes until top browns.

*To serve without freezing, bake in 350° F. oven for 15 minutes. Finish as directed.

cut out pulp leaving
a ¾ inch shell

EGGPLANT OREGANO

(8 to 10 servings)

Eggplants, cubed, 2 medium
Oil, 6 tablespoons
Garlic, crushed, 2 cloves
Onion, finely chopped, 2
Green pepper, sliced, 1
Orégano, 1 tablespoon

Brown sugar, 1 tablespoon
Wine vinegar, 2 tablespoons
Salt, 1 teaspoon
Pepper, 1 teaspoon
Pimiento, cut into pieces,
   2 4-oz. cans

Peel eggplant and cube. Boil cubes in salted water for 5 minutes. Drain. Put 2 tablespoons of oil in skillet. Sauté garlic for 1 minute. Add onions and pepper and sauté till wilted (about 5 minutes). Remove from pan. Add 4 tablespoons of oil and orégano to skillet and cook for 10 minutes over low heat. Add eggplant, sprinkle with sugar and cook over medium heat for 10 minutes, turning occasionally. Remove from heat. Sprinkle vinegar, salt and pepper over eggplant and mix well. Stir in garlic, onions and peppers. Put a layer of eggplant in bottom of casserole and dot with pimiento. Continue with layers until eggplant is used. Top with pimiento.* Cool. Wrap casserole. Freeze.

Serving day: Bake casserole, covered, in 375° F. oven for about 45 minutes or until very hot.

> **To serve without freezing, bake for 20 to 25 minutes.*

CLAM-STUFFED MACARONI

(6 to 8 servings)

STUFFING

Minced clams, 10½-oz. can
Parsley, minced, 2 tablespoons
Chives, minced, 2 tablespoons
Mushrooms, chopped and
   drained, ½ cup (3-oz. can)
Stale white bread, crumbled,
   2 slices (no crust)

Grated Parmesan cheese,
   3 tablespoons
Mozzarella cheese, ¼ pound
Ricotta cheese, 4 tablespoons
Salt, 1 teaspoon
Pepper, ⅛ teaspoon

Tufoli or Manicotti macaroni, 24

SAUCE

Olive or peanut oil, 3 tablespoons

Garlic, minced, 1 clove

Tomato purée, 2½ cups
  (1 lb. 4 oz. can)

Dried orégano, 1 tablespoon

Sugar, 1 teaspoon

Salt, ½ teaspoon

Black pepper, ¼ teaspoon

Mozzarella cheese, diced,
  ½ pound

Mushroom caps, sautéed, ½ cup
  (3 oz. can)

Butter, 4 tablespoons

Grated Parmesan cheese, 1 cup

1. Drain clams and reserve 1 tablespoon of liquid. Mix clams and the tablespoon of liquid with other stuffing ingredients.

2. Boil macaroni in large quantity of water. Drain and rinse with cold water. Stuff with mixture. If some macaroni breaks, spread on stuffing and fold over. Grease individual casseroles or large shallow casserole and lay macaroni in a single layer.

3. Heat oil and cook garlic over high heat for 1 minute. Add tomato purée, orégano, sugar, salt and pepper. Cook for 20 minutes.

4. Spoon sauce between and over macaroni in casserole. Pour remaining sauce into freezer container and freeze. Sprinkle mozzarella cheese, mushroom caps and butter over casserole.* Wrap and freeze.

Serving day: Remove casserole to room temperature 2 hours before serving. Bake uncovered at 375° F. for 45 minutes. Heat remaining sauce and serve separately with grated cheese.

*To serve without freezing bake for 30 minutes.

stuff
macaroni

lay macaroni in a
single layer

STUFFED MUSHROOMS FLORENTINE

(12 servings)

Frozen leaf spinach, 2 10-oz. packages or 3 pounds fresh, washed spinach
Large mushrooms, 36
Butter, 1¼ cups (2½ sticks)
Garlic, crushed, 3 cloves
Onions, finally chopped, 3
Fine bread crumbs, ½ cup
Salt, 1½ teaspoons
Pepper, ¼ teaspoon
Dry mustard, ⅛ teaspoon
Nutmeg, ½ teaspoon
Grated Parmesan cheese, 5 tablespoons

1. Cook spinach in small quantity of unsalted water. Drain very thoroughly. Purée in blender or food mill (should be 1½ cups). Reserve. Wash mushrooms. Remove stems, chop and reserve them.

2. Melt butter in skillet and cook garlic for 1 minute. Remove pan from fire. Dip mushroom caps into the melted butter until well-coated on all sides, and place them capside down on a cooky sheet. Reheat butter remaining in skillet and sauté onions and mushroom stems until very soft (about 10 minutes). Add to this the puréed spinach, bread crumbs, and seasoning and mix well. Fill the mushroom caps with mixture, mounding it high, and sprinkle with grated cheese.* Cool and freeze. When solidly frozen, pack in a freezer container.

Serving day: Bake on a greased shallow pan, uncovered, at 375° F. for 20 to 25 minutes.

*To serve without freezing, bake as directed for 15 minutes.

cap side down on cooky sheet

fill

sprinkle with cheese

BAKED POLENTA

(4 to 5 servings)

Water, 4 cups
Salt, 1 teaspoon
Yellow corn meal, 1 cup

Butter, ¼ pound
Grated Parmesan cheese, ½ cup

1. Stir together 1 cup cold water, salt and corn meal. Using the top of a double boiler, bring 3 cups of water to a boil over direct heat. Stir in the corn meal mixture gradually. Cook for five minutes. Place over boiling water and cook for 4 minutes, stirring occasionally. Pour into greased loaf pan and chill until hard.

slice
when firm

2. Remove from mold and slice with sharp knife or string. Place slices overlapping on greased shallow baking dish. Melt butter and pour over polenta. Sprinkle on cheese.* Cool. Wrap and freeze.

Serving day: Bake, uncovered, at 350° F. for 30 minutes.

*To serve without freezing, bake for 20 minutes.

POTATO-CHEESE ROLLS

(4 servings)

Potatoes, 2 medium
Cream, 2 tablespoons
Butter, 2 tablespoons
Egg, beaten, 1
Salt, ½ teaspoon
Pepper, ⅛ teaspoon

Garlic, crushed, 1 clove
Grated Romano or Parmesan
 cheese, 3 tablespoons
Parsley, minced, 1 tablespoon
Fine breadcrumbs or cornflake
 crumbs, ¼ cup

Boil potatoes till soft. Drain and mash. Whip potatoes with cream and butter till fluffy. Beat in egg, salt, pepper and garlic. Fold in cheese and parsley. Wet hands and shape into rolls, 2" long by 1" in diameter. Roll in crumbs.* Freeze on flat tray. When firm, pack in containers and freeze.

shape into rolls

Serving day: Bake uncovered at 400° F. for 30 minutes, turning once.

*To serve without freezing, bake for 15 to 20 minutes.

POTATO GNOCCHI

(about 24 servings)

Potatoes, 1 pound (3 or 4)	Eggs, 2
Water, ½ cup	Grated Swiss cheese, ¾ cup
Salt, 1 teaspoon	Chives, minced, ¼ cup
Butter, 8 tablespoons	Parsley, minced, ¼ cup
Flour, sifted, ½ cup	Paprika, ¼ teaspoon

1. Boil potatoes in well-salted water until tender. Drain, peel and mash. (Yields 2 cups.)

2. Heat water and salt in saucepan. Add 4 tablespoons of butter and bring to a boil. Add flour all at once and stir vigorously with a wooden spoon over low heat until mixture leaves the sides of the pan and forms a smooth ball. Transfer paste to large mixing bowl. Add eggs, 1 at a time, beating thoroughly until thick dough is formed. Beat in mashed potatoes, ¼ cup grated cheese, chives, parsley, and paprika. Chill for 30 minutes.

3. Take large spoonfuls of the dough, roll it with your hands on a floured board into cylinders about 1½" in diameter. Cut into 1½" lengths. Bring salted water to a boil in a large shallow pan (roaster) and reduce to a simmer. Poach gnocchi, uncovered, for 15 to 20 minutes, until they roll over easily in the water. Drain on a towel.* Cool. Freeze on a flat surface. Pack in container and freeze.

Serving day: Place frozen gnocchi on a greased baking dish. Melt 4 tablespoons of butter and spoon it over them. Sprinkle with ½ cup of grated Swiss cheese. Bake, uncovered, at 350° F. for 35 minutes.

> *To serve without freezing, bake as directed for 10 minutes.*

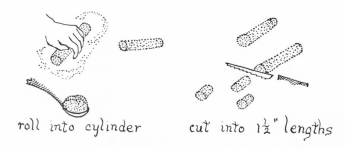

roll into cylinder   cut into 1½" lengths

RATATOUILLE

(8 servings)

Eggplant, peeled and cubed, 1 medium
Flour for dredging
Olive oil, ½ cup
Garlic, crushed, 2 cloves
Onion, chopped, 1
Zucchini, unpeeled and cut in ½" slices, 2
Green peppers, cut in strips, 2

Whole tomatoes, peeled, seeded and chopped, 4 (or 1 lb. can, drained)
Salt, 1½ teaspoons
Black pepper, ⅛ teaspoon
Basil, ¼ teaspoon
Orégano, ¼ teaspoon
Grated Parmesan cheese, ½ cup

Dredge eggplant very lightly in flour. Heat 3 tablespoons of oil in skillet and sauté eggplant on all sides, until golden brown. Remove. Add 3 tablespoons of oil to skillet and sauté garlic and onion until golden. Add zucchini and peppers and sauté for 5 minutes, stirring occasionally. Add tomatoes and seasoning. Simmer for 10 minutes. Grease a 2-quart casserole and place in it alternating layers of eggplant and the combined vegetables. Pour in remaining oil.* Cool. Wrap and freeze.

Serving day: Bake casserole, uncovered in 350° F. oven for 1½ hours. Five minutes before serving, sprinkle with grated cheese, increase heat to 450° F., and return casserole to oven until top is brown.

Note: Can be served cold as an appetizer or as a vegetable with charcoal-broiled steak, chops, etc. Defrost in refrigerator for 24 hours or at room temperature for about 6 hours. Omit cheese.

*To serve without freezing, bake at 350° F. for 45 minutes. Finish as directed.

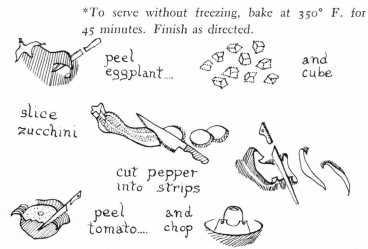

peel eggplant.... and cube

slice zucchini

cut pepper into strips

peel tomato.... and chop

FRIED RICE

(serves 4 to 6)

Cooked long-grained converted rice, 3 cups
Oil, 6 tablespoons
Eggs, lightly beaten, 3
Scallions, chopped, ½ cup

Water chestnuts, sliced, ¼ cup
Cooked ham, chopped, ¼ cup
Cooked lobster, chopped, ¼ cup
Chinese brown sauce
  (bead molasses), 1 teaspoon

1. Cook rice the day before or early in the morning and drain. Spread rice out on a flat pan and heat in a 250° F. oven until dry, stirring occasionally. Refrigerate overnight or in freezer for 45 minutes until cold but not frozen.

2. Heat oil in large skillet. Add rice and fry, stirring with a fork, for about 5 minutes until golden. Push rice away from the center to form a hollow. Pour eggs into hollow and scramble until only slightly set. Stir into rice until it's well coated. Stir in other ingredients and cook for 2 minutes, stirring constantly.* Spoon into shallow casserole and cool. Wrap and freeze.

pour eggs into hollow

Serving day: Heat at 350° F., uncovered, for 30 minutes until hot.

Note: If you want to double this recipe, use 2 skillets because you need room for all the stirring.

*Ready to serve without freezing.

RISOTTO MILANESE

(4 to 6 servings)

Butter, 6 tablespoons
Raw long-grained rice, 1 cup
Onion, chopped, 1
Garlic, crushed, 1 clove
Chicken broth, 2½ cups

Salt, 1 teaspoon
Saffron, ½ teaspoon
White wine, 2 tablespoons
Grated Parmesan cheese, ½ cup

Melt 4 tablespoons butter in heavy skillet. Stir in rice and cook over moderate heat till golden. Add onion and garlic. Cook over moderate heat for 5 minutes, stirring occasionally. Add 1 cup of broth and salt. Cook, covered, for 10 minutes. Dissolve saffron in wine and stir into rice. Add remaining broth and cook, covered, for 30 minutes.* Cool. Pour into casserole and freeze.

Serving day: Bake covered at 350° F. for 30 minutes. Stir in 2 tablespoons of butter and grated cheese. Bake for another 10 minutes.

> *To serve without freezing, stir in butter and cheese and serve.

RICE-NUT PILAF
(4 to 5 servings)

Butter, 2 tablespoons
Garlic, crushed, 3 cloves
Pignole nuts, 1 cup (or
    substitute sliced almonds)
Raw long-grained rice, 1 cup

Leek, chopped, 1
Chicken broth, 2½ cups
Salt, 1 teaspoon
Pepper, ½ teaspoon

Heat butter in skillet. Cook garlic for 1 minute. Add nuts and rice and cook about 4 minutes stirring frequently, until lightly browned. Add leek and cook 1 minute. Add 1 cup of broth, salt, and pepper and bring to a boil. Transfer rice to casserole. Bake at 375° F. for 25 minutes.* Cool and freeze.

Serving day: Thaw at room temperature for 1 hour. Stir in 1½ cups of broth. Bake at 375° F. for 1½ hours, stirring occasionally.

> *To serve without freezing, add remaining broth and bake for 45 minutes more.

ZUCCHINI MOUSSE au GRATIN
(serves 5 to 6)

Zucchini, 6 medium
Butter, 3 tablespoons
Scallions, finely chopped, 4
Fresh parsley, minced, ¼ cup
Fresh dill, minced, ¼ cup
Salt, 1½ teaspoon

Pepper, ⅛ teaspoon
Sour cream, ⅔ cup
Bread crumbs, 4 tablespoons
Grated Parmesan cheese,
    2 tablespoons

slice zucchini

1. Scrub zucchini, but do not peel. Cut up in small pieces. Steam, covered, in a strainer over boiling water until tender (about 20 minutes). Drain and shred with 2 knives and drain again.

2. Melt 1 tablespoon butter in a skillet and sauté scallions until wilted. Stir in zucchini, parsley, dill, salt, pepper and sour cream and cook a few minutes. Spoon mixture into a 1½ quart casserole. Top with bread crumbs, grated cheese, and dots of remaining 2 tablespoons butter.* Wrap and freeze.

Serving day: Bake, uncovered, at 375° F. for 1 hour and 15 minutes. Place under the broiler for 4 or 5 minutes to brown the top and serve.

*To serve without freezing, bake for 30 minutes. Brown as directed.

STUFFED ZUCCHINI FLORENTINE
(8 servings)

Zucchini, 8 small
Oil, ¼ cup
Lemon juice, 3 tablespoons
Bay leaf, 1
Fresh parsley, minced,
    1 tablespoon
Salt, 1½ teaspoons
Pepper, ¼ teaspoon
Frozen leaf spinach, 2 10-oz.
    packages or 3 lbs. fresh
    washed spinach.

Butter, 4 tablespoons
Garlic, crushed, 2 cloves
Onion, chopped, 4 small
Mushrooms, finely chopped, 1
    cup (less than ½ pound)
Italian-flavored bread crumbs,
    ½ cup
Grated Parmesan cheese, ¼ cup

cut in half lengthwise

scoop out seeds

1. Scrub zucchini, but do not peel. Cut in half lengthwise. Scoop out seeds with a melon-ball cutter, leaving a neat cavity to fill. Place in a large skillet: oil, lemon juice, bay leaf, parsley, 1 teaspoon salt, ⅛ teaspoon pepper and enough water to cover zucchini. Bring to a boil, put in zucchini and parboil for 2 minutes. Remove and drain, cut side down.

2. Cook spinach in a small amount of water. Drain very thoroughly. Purée in blender or food mill. Reserve (Yields ¾ cup.) Melt butter in a skillet and cook garlic for 1 minute. Add onions and mushrooms and sauté until soft (about 10 minutes). Add puréed spinach, breadcrumbs, ½ teaspoon salt and ⅛ teaspoon pepper and mix well. Fill zucchini with spinach mixture. Top with grated cheese.* Cool. Freeze on flat tray. When frozen, pack in container and store in freezer.

Serving day: Bake, uncovered, at 375° F. for 25 minutes.

To serve without freezing, bake for 10 minutes.

ZUCCHINI STUFFED WITH GREEN RICE
(serves 8 to 10)

Butter, ½ cup
Garlic, crushed, 4 cloves
Fresh parsley, minced, ½ cup
Fresh dill, minced, ½ cup
Salt, 1½ teaspoon
Pepper, ¼ teaspoon
Unconverted rice, cooked until
    very tender, 2½ cups

Egg, 1
Zucchini, 8 medium
Oil, ¼ cup
Lemon juice, 3 tablespoons
Thyme, ¼ teaspoon
Bay leaf, 1

1. Melt butter and cook garlic over moderate heat for 30 seconds. Add parsley, dill, ½ teaspoon salt, and ⅛ teaspoon pepper. Let stand for 5 minutes. Mix into rice. Beat egg lightly and mix thoroughly into rice. Cool in refrigerator.

2. Scrub zucchini but do not peel. Cut in half the long way and scoop out seeds with a melon-ball cutter, leaving a neat cavity to fill. Place in a large skillet: oil, lemon juice, 1 teaspoon salt, ⅛ teaspoon pepper, thyme, bay leaf and enough water to cover

zucchini. Bring to a boil, put in zucchini and parboil for 2 minutes. Remove and drain, cut side down. Fill zucchini cavities with rice mixture and pat it into neat mounds.* Place on a flat surface and freeze. When firm, pack in container and return to freezer.

Serving day: Bake, uncovered, at 375° F. for 25 minutes.

> *To serve without freezing, bake for 10 to 15 minutes.*

ZUCCHINI STUFFED WITH PEA PUREE

(12 to 16 servings)

drain, cut side down

Zucchini, 12 medium	Sour cream, ¼ cup
Oil, ¼ cup	Butter, 2 tablespoons
Lemon juice, 3 tablespoons	Shallots or scallions, 1 cup
Thyme, ¼ teaspoon	Paprika, ½ teaspoon
Bay leaf, 1	Nutmeg, ½ teaspoon
Salt, 2½ teaspoons	Dried dill weed, ½ teaspoon
Pepper, ¼ teaspoon	Walnuts, chopped, 1 cup
Frozen peas, 4 10-oz. packages	Parmesan cheese, grated, ½ cup

1. Scrub zucchini but do not peel. Cut in half lengthwise. Scoop out seeds with a melon-ball cutter, leaving a neat cavity to fill. Place in a large skillet: oil, lemon juice, thyme, bay leaf, 1 teaspoon salt, ⅛ teaspoon pepper and enough water to cover zucchini. Bring to a boil and parboil zucchini for 2 minutes. Remove and drain, cut side down.

2. Cook peas until tender. Drain and purée in blender with sour cream. (Yields 4 cups.) Melt butter and sauté shallots until wilted, stirring occasionally. Add pea purée, 1½ teaspoons salt, ⅛ teaspoon pepper, other seasoning and walnuts. Mix well. Fill zucchini cavities with mixture and top with grated cheese.* Place on a flat surface and freeze. Pack in container and return to freezer.

Serving day: Bake, uncovered, in 375° F. oven for 20 minutes.

> *To serve without freezing, bake for 10 minutes.*

desserts

9

HEAVENLY LEMON CREAM DESSERT

(10 to 12 servings)

Vanilla wafers, crushed, 1¾ cups
Sugar, 1½ cups
Lemon juice, 9 tablespoons
  (3 lemons)

Heavy cream, 3 cups
Eggs, separated, 6
Salt, ¼ teaspoon

1. Line bottom of ungreased 9″ spring form with 1 cup of crumbs. Dissolve sugar in lemon juice in large mixing bowl and stir thoroughly. Whip cream. Reserve.

2. Beat egg yolks slightly with salt. Add to lemon mixture and beat thoroughly for a few minutes, until thick and creamy. Fold in whipped cream. Beat egg whites till stiff but not dry and fold into mixture. Pour into spring form. Top with remaining crumbs. Wrap and freeze.

Serving day: Unmold onto serving platter in morning. Return to freezer. Transfer to refrigerator 2½ to 3 hours before serving.

HEAVENLY APRICOT DESSERT

(16 to 18 servings)

Dried apricots, 2 cups,
  11-oz. package
Chocolate wafers, crushed,
  1¾ cups
Eggs, separated, 6

Heavy cream, 3 cups
Sugar, ¾ cup
Lemon juice, 3 tablespoons
Salt, ¼ teaspoon

1. Place apricots in saucepan with cold water to cover. Bring to a boil and simmer for 20 minutes. Purée in blender or through sieve. Line bottom of ungreased 9″ spring form with 1 cup of crumbs.

2. Beat 3 egg whites until stiff. Reserve. Beat remaining 3 egg whites until foamy. Add apricot purée and beat well. Combine with stiffly beaten whites. Whip the cream. Reserve.

3. Dissolve sugar in lemon juice in large bowl. Stir thoroughly. Beat egg yolks slightly with salt. Add to sugar mixture and beat thoroughly for a few minutes, until thick and creamy. Fold in whipped cream and apricot mixture. Pour into spring form. Top with remaining crumbs. Wrap and freeze.

Serving day: Unmold into serving platter in morning. Return to freezer. Transfer to refrigerator 2½ to 3 hours before serving.

STRAWBERRY LADY FINGER CAKE
(16 to 18 servings)

Strawberries, crushed, 3 cups fresh or 6 frozen 10-oz. packages (thawed and drained)
Lemon juice, 2 tablespoons
Sugar, ½ cup
Salt, ¼ teaspoon
Gelatin, 2 tablespoons
Cold water, 4 tablespoons
Heavy cream, 3 cups
Lady fingers, 30

1. Stir together strawberries, lemon juice, sugar and salt. Soften gelatin in cold water. Place over simmering water and stir until dissolved. Stir into strawberries. Chill. When almost set, whip 2 cups of cream and fold in.

2. Split lady fingers and place them on the bottom and upright along the sides of a 3-quart spring form. Pour in a generous third of mix and spread evenly to the edges. Add a layer of lady fingers, then another generous third of mix. Add the third layer of lady fingers and the remainder of the mix. Put in refrigerator overnight.* Next day, wrap and freeze.

Night before or **Serving day:** Thaw in refrigerator 8 to 10 hours or overnight. Two hours or less before serving, remove from spring form. Whip remaining cup of cream and spread on top and sides of cake. Refrigerate until served.

> **To serve without freezing, remove from spring form and spread with whipped cream. Refrigerate until served.*

PINEAPPLE-LADY FINGER CAKE
(16 to 18 servings)

Eggs, separated, 6
Salt, ½ teaspoon
Sugar, 1 cup
Crushed pineapple, 5 cups
  (2 #2 cans)

Lemon juice, 4 tablespoons
Gelatin, 2 tablespoons
Cold water, 4 tablespoons
Heavy cream, 3 cups
Lady fingers, 30

1. Beat egg yolks with salt in top of double boiler. Add sugar gradually and beat until thick. Drain pineapple. Add juice and lemon juice to egg and sugar. Cook over simmering water until thickened. Stir in pineapple. Remove from heat. Soften gelatin in cold water and stir thoroughly into pineapple mixture. Pour into large mixing bowl and chill.

2. When almost set, beat egg whites until stiff and whip 2 cups of cream. Fold cream and then egg whites into pineapple mixture. Split lady fingers and place them on the bottom and upright along the sides of a 9" spring form. Pour in a generous third of mix and spread evenly to the edge. Add a layer of lady fingers, then another generous third of mix. Add the third layer of lady fingers and the remainder of the mix. Put in refrigerator overnight.* Next day, wrap and freeze.

Serving day: Thaw in refrigerator 8 to 10 hours or overnight. Two hours or less before serving remove from spring form. Whip 1 cup of cream and spread on top and sides of cake. Refrigerate until served.

> **To serve without freezing, remove from spring form and spread with whipped cream. Refrigerate until served.*

split ladyfingers ...
place on bottom and
sides of spring form

CHOCOLATE MOUSSE LADY FINGER CAKE

(16 to 18 servings)

pour mousse on lady fingers

Unsweetened chocolate, 4 squares (4 ounces)
Eggs, separated, 6
Granulated sugar, ¾ cup
Milk, ⅓ cup
Salt, ⅛ teaspoon

Butter, 1½ cups (¾ pound)
Confectioners' sugar, sifted, 1 cup
Vanilla, 1 teaspoon
Lady fingers, 30

Ingredients to be added Day of Party:
Heavy cream, 1 cup
Instant coffee, 1 teaspoon
Confectioners' sugar, 1 teaspoon

1. Melt chocolate in the top of a double boiler over hot water. Beat egg yolks till lemon-colored. Gradually beat in sugar till smooth and thick. Beat in milk. Add egg mixture to chocolate. Cook over hot water, stirring until well blended (5 or 10 minutes). Transfer to large mixing bowl and let cool for 30 minutes.

2. Beat egg whites with salt till stiff but not dry. Beat in ½ cup confectioners' sugar, a tablespoon at a time. Reserve. Cream butter. Gradually beat in rest of confectioners' sugar. Add to chocolate mix and stir until well blended. Gently fold in beaten whites and vanilla.

3. Line the bottom and sides of a 3-quart spring form with lady fingers (split and used singly). Pour in a generous third of mix and spread neatly to edges. Add a layer of lady fingers, then another generous third of mix. Add the third layer of lady fingers, and the remainder of the mix. Put in refrigerator overnight (for the mix to blend well with the lady fingers).* Next day, wrap and freeze.

Serving day: Thaw in refrigerator 8 to 10 hours or overnight. Two hours or less before serving, remove from spring form. Whip cream with coffee and sugar and spread on top and sides of cake. Refrigerate until served.

> *To serve without freezing, remove from spring form and spread with flavored whipped cream. Refrigerate until served.

APRICOT-MACAROON CAKE

Dried apricots, 4 cups
   (2 11-oz. packages)
Lemon juice, 2 tablespoons
Sugar, 1 cup
Salt, ¼ teaspoon

Gelatin, 2 tablespoons
Cold water, 4 tablespoons
Heavy cream, 3 cups
Soft macaroon crumbs, 8 cups
   (about 3 pounds)

1. Place apricots in a saucepan with cold water to cover. Bring to a boil and simmer for 20 minutes. Drain and purée in blender. (Yields 3 cups.) Stir together purée, lemon juice, sugar and salt. Soften gelatin in cold water. Place over simmering water and stir until dissolved. Stir into purée. Chill.

2. When well chilled, whip 2 cups of cream until stiff and fold in. Spread 3 cups of crumbs evenly on bottom of 9" spring form. Spoon in a generous third of the mix and spread evenly to the edges. Add an even layer of 2½ cups of crumbs, then another generous third of the mix. Add the remaining crumbs and remainder of mix. Refrigerate overnight.* Next day, wrap and freeze.

Serving day: Eight to ten hours before serving or the night before, place in refrigerator to thaw. Two hours or less before serving, remove sides of spring form, whip remaining cup of cream and spread on top and sides of cake. Decorate with a few canned apricot halves.

*To serve without freezing 2 hours or less before serving, remove sides of spring form and spread with whipped cream.

APRICOT MERINGUE TORTE
(12 to 14 servings)

MERINGUE

Egg whites, 8 (1 cup)
Salt, ¼ teaspoon
Cream of tartar, ½ teaspoon

Sugar, 2 cups
Almond extract, 2 teaspoons

Build rings around 3 circles
Press kisses around 4th

APRICOT CREAM FILLING

Dried apricots, 4 cups   Salt, ¼ teaspoon
  (2 11-ounce packages)   Gelatin, 2 tablespoons
Lemon juice, 2 tablespoons   Cold water, 4 tablespoons
Sugar, ¾ cup   Heavy cream, 2 cups

1. Beat egg whites until frothy. Add salt and cream of tartar. Beat until stiff but not dry and until mixture stands in peaks when beaters are withdrawn. Add sugar gradually, beating constantly. Fold in almond extract.

beat until mixture stands in peaks

2. Cover baking sheets with heavy, unglazed brown paper. Trace four circles 8″ in diameter, at least 1″ apart. With a pastry bag, build a ring around three of the circles, about 1½″ high, by laying several coils of meringue in layers one on top of another. With all but 2 tablespoons of the remaining meringue, press kisses around the fourth circle. Bake rings and kisses in 275° F. oven for 40 minutes.

3. With spatula, carefully remove rings and kisses from paper while still moist. Stack one ring on the other, sticking them to-gether with the unbaked meringue. Put back in warm oven (with heat off) for 1 hour. Reserve kisses. Remove ring Torte to serv-ing platter and cool. Fill with apricot cream and top cream with kisses.* Place in freezer. Wrap when frozen and freeze.

APRICOT CREAM FILLING

Place apricots in saucepan with cold water to cover. Bring to a boil and simmer for 20 minutes. Purée in blender or through sieve. Stir together apricot purée, lemon juice, sugar and salt. Soften gelatin in cold water. Place over simmering water and stir until dissolved. Stir into apricots. Refrigerate. When well chilled, whip cream until stiff and fold into purée.

Serving day: Transfer Torte to refrigerator 6 to 8 hours before serving.

To serve without freezing, refrigerate 3 hours.

BUCHE DE NOEL

(18 to 20 servings)

CAKE

Cake flour, 6 tablespoons

Cocoa, 6 tablespoons

Salt, ¼ teaspoon

Baking powder, ¾ teaspoon

Eggs, separated, 4

Sugar, ¾ cups

Vanilla, 1 teaspoon

Powdered sugar

SYRUP

Sugar, ¼ cup

Water, ¼ cup

Rum, ¼ cup

WHIPPED CREAM FILLING

Unsweetened Dutch cocoa,
    ¾ cup

Sugar, 1 cup

Instant demitasse coffee,
    2 tablespoons

Salt, pinch

Soft butter, 2 teaspoons

Hot water, ⅓ cup

Vanilla, ½ teaspoon

Almond extract, ½ teaspoon

Heavy cream, 3 cups

Pistachio nuts, chopped, ¼ cup

1. Sift flour, cocoa, salt and baking powder together 3 times. Beat egg whites till stiff but not dry. Gradually beat in half the sugar. Reserve. Beat egg yolks until thick and lemon colored. Add remaining sugar gradually and beat until creamy. Add vanilla. Gradually beat in dry ingredients until batter is smooth. Gently fold in the egg whites.

2. Grease a jelly roll pan 10″ x 15″ x ½″. Line with wax paper and grease again. Pour in batter and spread evenly. Bake in 375° F. oven for 12 to 13 minutes. (Do not *overbake*.) Sprinkle clean dish towel with powdered sugar. Loosen cake from sides of pan and invert on cloth. Remove wax paper and trim crisp edges of cake. Carefully roll up cake in cloth into a 15″ long roll. (The towel will be on the inside of cake.) Cool on rack for 30 minutes.

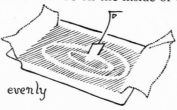

spread batter evenly   roll up cake in cloth

SYRUP

3. Combine sugar and water in saucepan. Cover and boil for 5 minutes. Add rum.

WHIPPED CREAM FILLING

4. In a bowl, mix together cocoa, sugar, coffee, salt, and butter. Pour in hot water to make a paste. Add vanilla and almond extract. Whip cream until stiff. Add cocoa mixture and mix well. Refrigerate until needed.

5. When cake is cool, carefully unroll and brush with half the syrup. Spread on ⅔ of whipped cream filling. Roll up cake. Cut off ends at a diagonal. Brush the outside of the cake with the remaining syrup, spread remaining whipped cream on top and sides, using a fork to give a bark-like appearance. (Or press out cream in ribbons through star of pastry bag.) Attach the cut-off end pieces to log as knots. Press into cream and cover with cream. Sprinkle with nuts.* Freeze until firm. Wrap and return to freezer.

Serving day: Remove to refrigerator 3 hours before serving. Serve in slices.

Ready to serve without freezing.

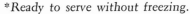

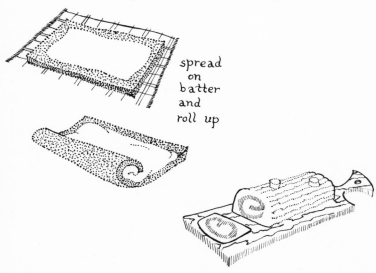

spread on batter and roll up

CHOCOLATE-DATE CAKE

Cake flour, sifted, 1¼ cups
plus 2 tablespoons
Pitted dates, ½ pound
Baking powder, 3 teaspoons
Salt, ¼ teaspoon
Bitter chocolate, 3½ ounces

Milk, 1 cup
Sugar, sifted, 2 cups
Eggs, separated, 4
Vanilla, ½ teaspoon
Orange rind, grated, 1 tablespoon
Walnuts, chopped, ½ cup

cut up dates
with wet scissors

1. Sprinkle 2 tablespoons of flour on wax paper. Cut dates with a scissors, as finely as possible, onto flour. Mix together. Reserve. Sift together 1¼ cups of flour, baking powder and salt. Reserve. Melt chocolate and milk in double boiler over hot water. Add 1 cup sugar and stir until smooth. Reserve.

2. Beat egg yolks in mixing bowl until light-colored. Gradually beat in remaining cup sugar until well blended. Stir in chocolate mixture. Stir in vanilla and sifted ingredients until well blended. Stir in dates, orange rind and walnuts. Beat egg whites until stiff and fold into mixture.

3. Pour into ungreased 9″ tube pan. Bake in 350° F. oven for 1 hour and 10 minutes. Cool in pan. When cool, remove from pan,* wrap and freeze.

Serving day: Thaw, wrapped at room temperature for 2 hours. Unwrap, and thaw for 1 hour more. Serve with whipped cream, Brandy Sauce, or as is.

*Ready to serve without freezing.

BRANDY CREAM SAUCE

(2 cups)

brandy

Butter, ½ cup
Confectioners' sugar, sifted,
1 cup
Salt, ⅛ teaspoon

Egg, separated, 1
Brandy, 2 tablespoons
Heavy cream, ½ cup

1. Cream butter and gradually beat in sugar until light-colored and fluffy. Beat in salt and egg yolk. Cook over hot water in a double boiler, stirring constantly, until thickened and creamy (about 5 minutes). Remove from heat and stir in brandy. Transfer to mixing bowl and chill.

2. Beat egg white until stiff. Whip cream. Fold egg white and cream into sauce.* Pour into container and freeze.

Serving day: Thaw in refrigerator for 6 hours or at room temperature for 2 hours.

Ready to serve without freezing.

PRUNE CAKE

Cake flour, 2½ cups
Baking powder, 3 teaspoons
Soda, 1 teaspoon
Salt, ½ teaspoon
Nutmeg, ½ teaspoon
Allspice, ¼ teaspoon
Butter, ¾ cup

Brown sugar, ½ cup
Granulated sugar, ½ cup
Eggs, 3
Prune pulp, puréed, 1⅔ cup
Sour cream, ¼ cup
Prune juice, ¾ cup
Chopped walnuts, 1 cup

thaw, wrapped, at room temperature

1. Sift together flour, baking powder, soda, salt, nutmeg and allspice. Reserve.

2. Cream butter and gradually add sugars, beating until light and fluffy. Beat in eggs, 1 at a time. Add prune pulp and beat well. At moderate speed, beat in flour mixture, alternating with sour cream and prune juice. Stir in nuts.

3. Grease and flour a 9" spring form pan. Pour in mixture and bake in 350° F. oven for 1 hour and 10 minutes. Cool in pan for 5 minutes; then remove and cool on a rack* Wrap and freeze.

Serving day: Thaw, wrapped, at room temperature for 1 hour. Serve with whipped cream.

Note: This can be baked in a 9" x 13" x 2" pan at 350° F. for 25 minutes.

Ready to serve without freezing.

CHEESE CAKE

(16 to 18 servings)

CRUST

Graham cracker crumbs, 1¼ cups	Sugar, 2 tablespoons
Ground almonds or walnuts, 4 tablespoons	Ground lemon peel, 1 teaspoon
	Melted butter, ½ cup

FILLING

Soft cream cheese, 1½ pounds	Lemon juice, 3 teaspoons
Sugar, 1 cup	Lemon rind, 1 teaspoon
Vanilla, 1 teaspoon	Eggs, 4

TOPPING

cool in oven
with door open

Ice-cold sour cream, 1 pint	Vanilla, ½ teaspoon
Sugar, ½ cup	

1. Combine crumbs, nuts, sugar and lemon peel. Stir in butter until thoroughly blended. Press mixture firmly against bottom of 9″ spring form. Bake in 350° F. oven for 10 minutes.

2. In large bowl of mixer, beat cheese until creamy. At medium speed, add sugar gradually, then vanilla, lemon juice and rind and blend well. Add eggs, 1 at a time, and beat at medium speed for 10 minutes, until fluffy. Pour into pan. Bake at 250° F. for 35 minutes. Turn off heat and cool for 30 minutes in oven with door open.

3. Combine sour cream, sugar and vanilla and whip for 10 minutes, until foamy. Spoon over top of cake. Bake in 250° F. oven for 10 minutes. Sprinkle with cinnamon. Cool.* Wrap. Freeze.

Serving day: Remove from spring form and thaw in refrigerator for 4 or 5 hours.

*To serve without freezing, refrigerate for 2 hours or more before unmolding.

BABA AU RHUM

(24 individual muffins or 1 mold of 2 quarts)

Milk, ¼ cup	Sugar, 2 tablespoons
Dried currants, ¾ cup	Soft butter, ½ cup
Rum, 2 tablespoons	Eggs, 3 (at room temperature)
Ginger, ⅛ teaspoon	Salt, ½ teaspoon
Warm water, ¼ cup	Grated lemon rind, 1 tablespoon
Dry yeast, 1 package	Apricot-Rum Syrup
Flour, sifted, 2 cups	(recipe follows)

1. Scald milk and cool to lukewarm. Rinse currants and let soak in rum. Combine ginger and warm water in a small bowl. Sprinkle on yeast and stir until dissolved. Let stand in a warm place until thickened (about 3 or 4 minutes). Mix together ½ cup of flour, 1 tablespoon sugar and warm milk. Add yeast mixture and beat well with a wooden spoon until smooth. Cover and let rise in a warm place for about 45 minutes or until doubled.

spoon into well-greased

individual baba molds

2. Cream butter and remaining tablespoon of sugar. Beat eggs and stir into butter with salt, lemon rind and currants. Stir in flour until it is absorbed. Add yeast sponge and beat very well with a wooden spoon for 5 or 10 minutes. Spoon into very well greased individual baba molds or muffin tins, or into a 2-quart ring or baba mold, filling half full. Cover with a cloth and let rise in a warm place 1 hour or until risen to top of mold.

or muffin tins

or a 2-quart mold filling half-way

3. Bake in 350° F. oven, 20 minutes for individual cakes and 25 minutes for large mold. Remove from pans and cool on cake rack.* Wrap in bags and freeze.

Serving day: Two or three hours before serving, remove the babas from the freezer. Wrap in foil or a brown paper bag and heat at 350° F. for 4 or 5 minutes. Place warm cakes in wide shallow dish and pour warm Apricot-Rum syrup over them. Let them soak for 2 hours. Serve, covered with puréed apricot jam and with whipped cream or as is. To flambé, sprinkle cakes with confectioners' sugar. Pour over them ½ cup warm rum and ignite.

To serve without freezing, soak for 2 hours before serving.

APRICOT RUM SYRUP

Sugar, 1½ cups   Lemon juice, 1 tablespoon
Apricot nectar, 3 cups   Rum, ¾ cup

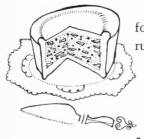

Combine sugar and apricot nectar. Bring to a boil and cook for 10 minutes. Remove from fire and stir in the lemon juice and rum.

APPLE CHARLOTTE

(9" spring form — 12 to 14 servings)

PASTRY

Flour, sifted, 3 cups   Lemon, 1
Shortening, 1 cup   Sugar, ½ cup
Egg yolks, 2   Egg, separated, 1
Ice water, ¼ cup

FILLING

Cornflake crumbs, 1 cup   Cinnamon, 1 teaspoon
Tart, firm apples, coarsely grated, Seedless raisins, 1 cup
   9 cups   Dried currants, ½ cup
Lemon, 1   Sherry, ¼ cup
Sugar, 1 cup

PASTRY

1. Cut shortening into sifted flour. Beat 2 egg yolks and water with a fork. Add to flour mixture, pressing particles together with a fork, until all are moistened. Squeeze juice from lemon and grate rind. Add to mixture. Stir in sugar. Gather dough together and press into a firm ball. Chill for 30 minutes.

2. Cut off ¼ of dough and reserve in refrigerator for top crust. On lightly floured board, roll out remainder of dough about ⅜" thick and large enough to fit into a 9" spring form. Lift carefully and fit loosely into the pan. If it breaks, fill in broken sections with dough and firmly press parts together and into sides of pan. Trim edge even with rim. Prick bottom in a few places with fork and brush with 1 lightly beaten egg white. Bake crust on lower shelf of 475° F. oven for 8 minutes. Cool. Place in freezer for 1 hour or longer.

FILLING

3. Spread ½ cup of crumbs over frozen bottom crust. Squeeze juice from lemon and grate rind. Sprinkle over grated apples. Combine remaining crumbs, sugar, cinnamon, raisins, currants and sherry and stir gently into apples. Fill the frozen crust with apple mixture and cover with remaining dough, rolled out ¼" thick. Seal edges. Beat egg yolk with a little milk and brush on top crust.* Wrap. Freeze.

Serving day: Bake on bottom shelf in 500° F. oven for 15 minutes. Reduce heat to 425° F., move cake to upper shelf and bake for 1 hour. Sprinkle with sugar and serve at room temperature.

> *To serve without freezing, bake on lower shelf in 450° F. oven for 15 minutes. Reduce heat to 400° F., move to upper shelf and bake for 45 minutes.

fit pastry into pan

if it breaks,

fill in with dough and press together

APPLESAUCE TART
(9" pie)

PASTRY

Flour, sifted, 1½ cups
Salt, ¼ teaspoon
Sugar, ¼ cup
Grated lemon peel, ½ teaspoon

Soft butter, ½ cup
Egg yolks, 2
Lemon juice, 1 tablespoon
Egg white, 1

work with fingers into a paste

FILLING

Green apples, 3 pounds
Water, 3 tablespoons
Butter, 2 tablespoons
Grated lemon peel, ½ teaspoon
Sugar, ½ cup
Red baking apples, 2

Lemon juice, ½ cup
Vanilla, 1 teaspoon
Walnuts, chopped, ½ cup
Apricot preserves, ½ cup
Apricot brandy, 2 tablespoons

1. Sift flour and salt into a large bowl. Make a well in the center and put the sugar, lemon peel, butter and egg yolks. With fingertips of one hand, work center ingredients into a smooth paste. Gradually work in the flour. Sprinkle on lemon juice, pressing particles together with a fork until all are moistened. Gather the dough up into a ball, working it together until smooth. Wrap in wax paper and chill for 15 minutes.

2. Roll out into a circle 1" larger than the diameter of the pan. Press into pan, trim and flute edges. Brush with lightly beaten egg white. Bake in 375° F. oven for 7 minutes. Cool and freeze for 1 hour or more.

3. Peel and thinly slice green apples. Place in a heavy saucepan with water, butter and lemon peel. Cover and simmer for 15 minutes. Stir in sugar over low heat and cook for 5 minutes. Drain, reserving juice, and cool thoroughly.

arrange apples in overlapping circles

4. Peel and thinly slice red apples. Soak them in lemon juice and vanilla for 15 to 30 minutes. Spread chopped walnuts over frozen pastry shell. Fill with cooled applesauce, heaping it high in the middle. Drain raw apples and arrange in overlapping circles on top of applesauce. Spoon on reserved applesauce juice.* Wrap in foil and freeze.

Serving day: Bake frozen pie on a lower shelf in 450° F. oven for 20 minutes. Reduce heat to 375° F. and bake for 35 minutes. Heat together apricot preserves and brandy and stir until dissolved. Pour over apples while pie is still hot. Serve cool or chilled, with whipped cream, brandy cream or as is.

*To serve without freezing, bake as directed, reducing time in 375° F. oven to 20 to 25 minutes.

APPLE PIE
(9″ pie)

arrange apples, cut side down

PASTRY

Flour, sifted, 2 cups
Salt, 1 teaspoon
Lemon peel, grated, 1 tablespoon
Lard or vegetable shortening, chilled, ⅔ cup

Ice water, 2 tablespoons
Lemon juice, chilled, 2 tablespoons
Egg, separated, 1

FILLING

Cornflake crumbs, ¼ cup
Flour, 4 tablespoons
Brown sugar, ½ cup
Salt, ⅛ teaspoon
Tart, firm apples, peeled and quartered, 6 cups (about 7 apples)

Lemon juice, 1 tablespoon
Grated lemon peel, 1 tablespoon
Apple brandy, 3 tablespoons
Currants, ½ cup
Butter, 2 tablespoons

1. Add salt to sifted flour and sift again. Mix with lemon rind. Cut in shortening until particles are the size of peas. Sprinkle on water and lemon juice a little at a time. With a fork, press moistened particles together until dough forms. Turn out on wax paper and form into 2 balls. Chill in refrigerator for 30 minutes.

2. Roll out one portion ⅛″ thick into a circle 1″ larger than diameter of pan. Place in pan and trim edge. Brush with lightly beaten egg white. Place in freezer for 1 hour or more.

3. Spread crumbs over frozen bottom crust. Combine flour, sugar and salt. Mix apples with lemon juice, lemon peel, brandy and currants. Place apple mixture in pie, cut sides down, inter-

spersing with sprinklings of the flour mixture. Dot with butter.

4. Roll out remaining dough for top crust. Place on top of pie and seal edges, fluting to make a standing rim. Brush with egg yolk diluted with a little milk.* Freeze. Wrap when firm and return to freezer.

Serving day: Prick crust and bake on lower shelf in a 500° F. oven for 15 minutes. Reduce heat to 450° F. and bake for 45 minutes until browned. Sprinkle with sugar and serve warm or at room temperature.

> *To serve without freezing, prick crust and bake on a lower shelf, at 425° F. for 40 to 45 minutes.*

VERY HIGH PEACH PIE
(9")

PASTRY

Flour, sifted, 2 cups	Ice water, 2 tablespoons
Salt, 1 teaspoon	Lemon juice, chilled,
Lemon rind, 1 tablespoon	2 tablespoons
Shortening, chilled, ⅔ cup	Egg yolk, separated, 1

FILLING

Graham cracker crumbs, ½ cup	Lemon juice, 1 tablespoon
Flour, 5 tablespoons	Grated lemon rind, 2 tablespoons
Brown sugar, ½ cup	Peach brandy, 2 tablespoons
Salt, ⅛ teaspoon	Butter, 2 tablespoons
Fresh peaches, peeled and halved, 6 cups (about 14 peaches)	

1. Add salt to sifted flour and sift again. Mix with lemon rind. Cut in shortening until particles are the size of peas. Sprinkle water and lemon juice a little at a time. With a fork, press moistened particles together until dough forms. Turn out on wax paper and form into 2 balls. Chill in refrigerator for 30 minutes.

2. Roll out 1 portion, ⅛" thick, into a circle 1" larger than diameter of pan. Place in pan and trim edge. Brush with lightly beaten egg white. Place in freezer for 1 hour or more.

3. Spread crumbs over frozen bottom crust. Combine flour, sugar and salt. Sprinkle peaches with lemon juice, lemon rind and brandy. Arrange peaches, cut side down, in layers, interspersing with sprinklings of flour mixture. Dot with butter.

4. Roll out remaining dough for top crust. Place on top of pie and seal edges, fluting to make a standing rim. Brush with egg yolk, diluted with a little milk.* Freeze. Wrap when firm and return to freezer.

Serving day: Prick crust with fork and bake on lower shelf in 500° F. oven for 15 minutes. Reduce heat to 450° F., and bake for 45 minutes, until browned. Sprinkle with sugar and serve warm or at room temperature.

To serve without freezing, prick crust and bake on a lower shelf in 425° F. oven for 40 to 45 minutes.

arrange peaches,
cut side down

FRUIT-NUT BARS
(about 60)

flute edges

Seedless raisins, rinsed and drained, ½ cup	Eggs, 2
Dried apricots, chopped, ½ cup	Rum, 1 teaspoon
Raspberry jam, 2 cups	Nutmeg, ¼ teaspoon
Chopped walnuts, 2 cups	Flour, 2 cups

Blend well all ingredients except flour. Gradually add flour and mix thoroughly. Grease a shallow baking pan (11″ x 15″). Spread mixture about ½″ thick. Bake at 300° F. for 35 minutes. Cool.* Place pan in freezer for 1 hour. When firm, cut into 1½″ x 1½″ pieces. Pack into container and freeze.

Serving day: Thaw at room temperature for 30 minutes.

To serve without freezing, cut into pieces.

RUM BALLS
(makes about 70)

Vanilla wafers, crushed, 1 cup
Walnuts or pecans, chopped,
  1½ cups
Powdered sugar, 1 cup

Cocoa, 2 tablespoons
Corn syrup, light, 2 tablespoons
Rum, ¼ cup
Chocolate sprinkles, 1 cup

form into balls

Crush vanilla wafers and chop nuts. Combine with sugar and cocoa. Stir in corn syrup and rum. Wet hands and form mixture into balls the size of large olives. Roll in chocolate sprinkles. Freeze on flat tray. When firm, pack in container.

Serving day: Keep frozen till ready to serve.

RASPBERRY OR CHERRY CRESCENTS
(about 30)

Cream cheese, ½ cup (4 ounces)
Butter, ½ cup (¼ pound)
Flour, sifted, 1 cup
Salt, ¼ teaspoon

Raspberry or cherry preserves,
  ½ cup
Walnuts, chopped, ½ cup
Grated lemon peel, 2 teaspoons
Egg yolk, 1

1. Soften cheese and butter and cream together with a spoon. Gradually work in flour and salt until well blended. Form into a ball. Chill for 1 hour in freezer or 4 hours to overnight in refrigerator.

2. Cut dough in half. Roll out both halves into rectangles, each about ⅛″ thick. Cut into 2″ squares. Cut each square into a triangle.

3. Mix together preserves, nuts, and lemon peel. Place about ½ teaspoon of preserves in center of wide edge. Roll up, starting with wide edge. Shape into a crescent.

4. Beat egg yolk slightly with milk and brush on pastry. Bake in 350° F. oven on upper shelf for 15 to 20 minutes, until lightly

browned.* Cool. Freeze on flat surface. When frozen, pack in containers with freezer paper between layers. Return to freezer.

Serving day: Thaw at room temperature for 30 minutes. Dust with confectioners' sugar.

Ready to serve without freezing.

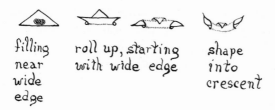

filling near wide edge   roll up, starting with wide edge   shape into crescent

FUDGE BROWNIES
(32 1″ x 2″ bars)

Bitter chocolate, 2 squares	Flour, ½ cup
Butter, ½ cup	Salt, pinch
Sugar 1 cup	Chopped walnuts, ½ cup
Eggs, 2	

1. Melt chocolate and butter over simmering water. Cool in large mixing bowl. Beat in sugar gradually. Add eggs, 1 at a time, and beat well. Add remaining ingredients and mix well.

2. Grease and flour an 8″ or 9″ square pan. Pour in the batter. Bake in a 350° F. oven for 25 to 30 minutes. Cool.* Chill for 1 hour in freezer. Cut into bars. Pack in a container with freezer paper between the layers. Return to freezer.

Serving day: Thaw at room temperature for 30 minutes.

To serve without freezing, cut into bars.

PROFITEROLLES
CREAM PUFFS

(about 32 puffs)

Water, 1 cup	Eggs, 5
Butter, ½ cup	Milk, ½ teaspoon
Sugar, 1 teaspoon	Filling and Sauce recipes
Salt, ½ teaspoon	(see index)
Flour, sifted, 1 cup	

1. Heat water in saucepan. Add butter and melt. Add sugar and salt and bring to a boil. Reduce heat and add flour all at once. Stir vigorously with a wooden spoon, over low heat, until mixture leaves the sides of the pan and forms a smooth ball. Transfer to mixing bowl. Add 4 eggs, one at a time, beating thoroughly after each addition, until thick dough is formed.

2. Place rounded teaspoonfuls of batter on an ungreased baking sheet, 2" apart. Brush tops with 1 egg beaten with milk. Bake at 400° F. for 10 minutes. Reduce heat to 300° F., *without opening* oven door, and bake for 25 minutes.

cut slit in one side of puff

3. When cool, cut a slit in one side of each puff and fill with ice cream, flavored Whipped Cream, or Bavarian Cream.* (See following recipes.) Freeze on flat tray or cookie sheet. When firm, pack in freezer bags or container and store in freezer.

Serving day: Thaw at room temperature. Whipped cream or ice cream filled puffs will take ½ hour. Bavarian cream puffs will take 45 minutes to 1 hour. Serve with chocolate mint sauce or hot chocolate rum sauce.

Ready to serve without freezing.

WHIPPED CREAM FILLING
FOR CREAM PUFFS

Heavy cream, 1 cup	Cointreau or crème de menthe,
Confectioners' sugar, 2 teaspoons	2 teaspoons

Whip cream. Fold in sugar and liquor.

BAVARIAN CREAM FILLING FOR CREAM PUFFS

(makes 2½ cups)

Milk, 1⅓ cups	Salt, ¼ teaspoon
Gelatin, 1 tablespoon	Eggs, separated, 2
Water, 2 tablespoons	Heavy cream, 1 cup
Sugar, ½ cup	Vanilla, 1 teaspoon

1. Heat milk in top of double boiler. Remove from heat. Soften gelatin in water. Add to hot milk with sugar and salt. Stir till dissolved. Beat yolks slightly. Stir into remaining mixture. Cook over hot water, stirring until slightly thickened (about 5 minutes). Pour mixture into large mixing bowl. Chill until it begins to set.

2. Beat egg whites until stiff, and whip cream. Fold into mixture with vanilla. Place in refrigerator for 1 hour before filling puffs.

CHOCOLATE RUM BAVARIAN CREAM FOR CREAM PUFFS

Add 2 squares of unsweetened chocolate to milk before heating. When melted, beat well. Increase sugar to ⅔ cup. Substitute 2 teaspoons rum for vanilla.

CHOCOLATE MINT SAUCE FOR CREAM PUFFS

(2 cups)

Chocolate covered thin mints, 2 7-oz. boxes	Water, ½ cup
	Evaporated milk, ⅓ cup

Melt mints in water over medium heat. Stir in milk. Heat till blended. Pour into freezer containers and freeze.

Night before or **Serving day:** Defrost in refrigerator overnight or at room temperature for 6 hours. Serve cold.

HOT CHOCOLATE RUM SAUCE FOR CREAM PUFFS

(2 cups)

Bitter chocolate, 1 ounce
Sweet chocolate, 12 ounces

Water, ¾ cup
Rum, 2 tablespoons

Melt chocolate with water, stir till dissolved. Add rum.

CROQUEMBOUCHE—PYRAMID OF CREAM PUFFS

about 32 puffs (12 servings)

Cream Puffs, 1 recipe
Bavarian Cream, 1 recipe

Sugar, 1½ cups
Water, 1 cup

1. Bake cream puffs as directed. Fill with Bavarian Cream. Freeze on flat tray. When firm, pack in plastic bags or containers.

2. In a heavy saucepan, boil sugar and water. Stir till sugar dissolves. Cook over low heat without stirring till mixture thickens into a golden caramel syrup (about 30 minutes). Remove from heat. (Can be done ahead.)

3. One hour before serving, reheat syrup and build the cream puff pyramid. Arrange a 9″ circle of puffs on a serving platter by dipping the sides of 8 or 9 puffs into hot syrup and attaching them to each other, side by side. Dip the bottoms of the second row of puffs into the hot syrup and place on top of the first row, bridging the spaces between the puffs. Continue to build up puffs into a hollow pyramid shape, dipping the bottom of each puff into the syrup. Finish with 1 small puff on top and a sprinkling of confectioners' sugar.

4. At dessert time, pick off 2 or 3 puffs per portion and serve with chocolate mint sauce or hot chocolate rum sauce. Can be used as a centerpiece on buffet table.

CREME de MENTHE ALASKA PIE
(9")

CRUST

Chocolate (cooky) crumbs,
  1½ cups

Walnuts, chopped, ¼ cup
Butter, melted, ½ cup

FILLING

Vanilla ice cream, ½ gallon
Crème de menthe, ½ cup

Chocolate-mint (cooky) crumbs,
  2 cups

MERINGUE

Egg whites, 4
Salt, pinch
Cream of tartar, ¼ teaspoon

Granulated sugar, ½ cup
Crème de menthe, 2 teaspoons

CRUST

1. Mix together crumbs, walnuts, and butter until well blended. Press firmly into bottom and sides of 9" pie pan. Bake in 350° F. oven for 8 minutes. Cool. Freeze till firm.

FILLING

2. Put 1 pint of ice cream into frozen shell and spread in an even layer. Pour 2 tablespoons crème de menthe over ice cream, and top with ½ cup of crumbs. Repeat procedure in 3 more layers, ending with a topping of crumbs. Put in freezer until firm.

MERINGUE

3. Beat egg whites with salt until frothy. Add cream of tartar and beat until stiff but not dry. Gradually beat in sugar until glossy. Fold in crème de menthe.

4. Spread meringue over ice cream, sealing edges carefully to enclose ice cream. Place pie on a bread board and brown in 450° F. oven for 4 or 5 minutes. Immediately place in freezer. When frozen, wrap and return to freezer.

Serving day: Thaw at room temperature for 15 minutes before serving.

Note: The baked meringue top will not keep well in the freezer for more than one day. You can make the pie, except for the topping, at any time, adding and baking the meringue the day of, or the day before the party.

CHOCOLATE-COFFEE BOMBE
3 quarts (about 18 servings)

CHOCOLATE-RUM MOUSSE

Sugar, 1 cup
Dark Dutch cocoa, 9 tablespoons
Water, 6 tablespoons
Egg yolks, 6

Salt, ¼ teaspoon
Heavy cream, 3 cups
Rum, 6 tablespoons

COFFEE-KALHUA MOUSSE

Sugar, 1 cup
Instant demi-tasse coffee,
  4 tablespoons
Water, ⅓ cup
Egg yolks, 6

Salt, ¼ teaspoon
Heavy cream, 3 cups
Kalhua (or other coffee liquor),
  ½ cup

CHOCOLATE MOUSSE

spoon coffee mousse over chocolate lining

1. Combine sugar and cocoa in a saucepan. Stir in water. Bring to a boil and cook, without stirring, to the soft-ball stage.*

2. Beat yolks and salt until pale and thick. Add chocolate syrup in a fine stream, while beating. Continue beating until mixture forms peaks. Chill.

3. Whip the cream. Stir rum into mixture and then fold in cream. Spoon into chilled 3-quart mold. Using the back of the spoon, draw the Mousse up the sides of the mold and press to form an even layer on bottom and sides, leaving the center hollow. Place in freezer.

COFFEE MOUSSE

4. Combine sugar and coffee in 2-quart saucepan. Add water, Stir over low heat until sugar is dissolved. Bring to a boil and cook, without stirring, to the soft-ball stage.*

5. Beat egg yolks and salt until pale and thick. Add coffee syrup in a fine stream, while beating. Continue beating until mixture almost forms peaks. Chill.

6. Whip the cream. Stir Kalhua into mixture and then fold in cream. Spoon Coffee Mousse over frozen chocolate lining and fill to the top of the mold. Wrap in foil. Freeze.

Serving day: One or two hours before the party, unmold Bombe by dipping it into hot water for 10 seconds and inverting it onto a chilled serving tray. Return to freezer until serving time. Serve with whipped cream.

*Note: Soft-ball stage is 236° F. on a candy thermometer. Without a thermometer, the test is to spoon a few drops of syrup into cold water. If a mass collects, which can then be formed into a soft-ball with the fingers, it is ready.

drop a spoonful of
syrup into cold water

syrup cools and thickens
into a mass which can
be gathered up into
a pliable ball

CRÈME DE MENTHE—CHOCOLATE BOMBE

3 quarts (about 18 servings)

Sugar, 1 cup
Water, 1 cup
Egg yolks, 6
Salt, ¼ teaspoon
Heavy cream, 3 cups
Crème de menthe, ½ cup

Green food coloring, ¼ teaspoon
Chocolate mint wafers (candy),
  coarsely chopped, ¼ cup
Chocolate-Rum Mousse
  (see index)

1. Combine sugar and water in a 2-quart saucepan. Stir over low heat until sugar is dissolved. Bring to a boil and cook slowly, without stirring, to the soft-ball stage.

2. Beat egg yolks with salt until pale and thick. Add syrup in a fine stream while beating. Continue beating until mixture forms peaks. Chill.

3. Whip cream until stiff. Stir crème de menthe, food coloring and chopped chocolate into egg mixture and then fold in whipped cream. Spoon into chilled 3-quart mold. Using the back of spoon, draw the Mousse up the sides of the mold and press to form an even layer on bottom and sides, leaving the center hollow. Place in freezer.

4. Spoon Chocolate Mousse over frozen Crème de Menthe Mousse and fill to the top of the mold. Wrap in foil. Freeze.

Serving day: One or two hours before the party, unmold bombe by dipping it into hot water for 10 seconds and inverting it onto a chilled serving tray. Return to freezer until serving time. Serve with whipped cream.

release
vacuum
with
knife

dip mold into
hot water for
10 seconds

invert
onto
serving
platter

FROZEN PISTACHIO AND CHOCOLATE BOMBE

3 quarts (18 servings)

Pistachio ice cream,   Chocolate Mousse, 6 cups
  3 pints   (see index)

Chill a 3-quart mold. Spread the interior with a 1″ layer of ice cream using the back of a spoon to pack it down evenly. Set mold in freezer for 30 minutes to harden. Spoon the Mousse into the center up to the top of the mold. Freeze. When frozen, cover with foil.

Serving day: Unmold Bombe by dipping into hot water for 10 seconds. Loosen sides with knife and invert onto serving tray. Return to freezer. Thaw at room temperature for 15 minutes before serving. Slice with silver knife dipped into hot water. Serve with whipped cream.

FROZEN PINEAPPLE DELIGHT

1 quart (6 servings)

Eggs, separated, 3   Crushed pineapple, 9 oz. can
Salt, dash   Lemon juice, 2 tablespoons
Sugar, ½ cup plus 2 tablespoons   Heavy cream, 1 cup

1. Beat egg yolks with salt. Add ½ cup sugar gradually and beat until thick. Drain pineapple juice from can and mix with lemon juice. Fold into egg and sugar. Heat mixture in top of double boiler over simmering water. Stir until spoon is coated. Stir in pineapple. Transfer to large mixing bowl and cool.

2. Beat egg whites until stiff but not dry. Gradually beat in remaining 2 tablespoons of sugar until smooth. Whip cream. Fold cream and then egg white into pineapple mixture. Pour into 2 freezer trays. Freeze until firm, about 2 hours. Remove from freezer. Break up with a spoon and pack down firmly into quart container. Return to freezer.

Serving day: With ice cream scoop, shape into balls and place in a serving bowl or sherbet dishes. Keep in freezer until ready to serve. Serve with lady fingers and whipped cream.

FROZEN STRAWBERRY DELIGHT

makes 1 quart (6 to 8 servings)

Eggs, separated, 3
Salt, dash
Sugar, ½ cup plus 2 tablespoons
Frozen sliced strawberries,
  thawed, 2 10-ounce packages

Strawberry juice, ¼ cup
Lemon juice, 2 tablespoons
Kirsch, 3 tablespoons
Heavy cream, 1 cup

STRAWBERRY SAUCE

Currant jelly, ¼ cup
Strawberry juice (reserved from
  Delight recipe)

Frozen strawberries, crushed,
  10-oz. package
Kirsch, ¼ cup

1. Beat egg yolks with salt. Add ½ cup of sugar gradually, and beat until thick. Drain thawed berries. Mix ¼ cup of juice with lemon juice and fold into egg and sugar. (Reserve remainder of juice for sauce.) Heat mixture in top of double boiler over simmering water. Stir until spoon is coated. Crush the drained strawberries and stir in. Transfer to large mixing bowl and cool. Stir in Kirsch.

2. Beat egg whites until stiff but not dry. Gradually beat in remaining 2 tablespoons of sugar until smooth. Whip the cream. Gently fold cream and then egg white into berry mixture. Pour into 2 freezer trays. Freeze till firm (about 2 hours). Remove from freezer, break up with a spoon, and pack down firmly into quart container. Return to freezer.

SAUCE

3. Heat jelly with juice over low heat. Cool. Add berries and Kirsch. Freeze.

Serving day: With ice cream scoop, shape into balls and place in serving dish. Keep in freezer until ready to use. Serve with lady fingers and strawberry sauce. Thaw sauce at room temperature for 6 hours, or in refrigerator overnight.

FROZEN PEACH DELIGHT

Substitute 2 12-oz. packages of frozen peaches for the strawberries,
3 tablespoons peach brandy for the Kirsch

PEACH SAUCE

Orange marmalade, ¼ cup
Peach juice (reserved from
  Delight recipe)

Frozen peaches, crushed,
  12-oz package
Peach brandy, ¼ cup

Heat marmalade with juice over low heat. Cool. Add peaches
and brandy. Freeze.

PARFAIT-FILLED CHOCOLATE COLETTES

(16)

Semi-sweet chocolate bits, 2 cups
  (12-oz. package)
Butter, 4 tablespoons
Orange-flavored gelatin, 1 package
Orange juice, 1 cup

Vanilla ice cream, 1 pint
Orange Curaçao or apricot
  brandy, ¼ cup
Flaked coconut, ¼ cup

1. Melt chocolate with butter over hot water. Cool slightly.
Using 32 very small (tea size) fluted paper baking cups, put together 16 doubles. With the back of a spoon, spread melted
chocolate on bottom and sides of paper cup. Place filled paper
cups in a muffin pan and place in freezer.

2. Heat orange juice in a 2-quart saucepan. Dissolve orange
gelatin in it. Gradually add ice cream by spoonfuls, stirring until
melted. Stir in Curaçao or brandy. Chill in refrigerator until thickened (about 30 minutes).

peel off paper

3. Spoon into frozen chocolate cups. Sprinkle top with flaked coconut.* Return to freezer. When frozen, pack in container in layers. (They will not stick to each other.)

Serving day: Thaw in refrigerator for 20 minutes. Peel off paper gently. Place in fresh paper cups and return to refrigerator until ready to serve.

To serve without freezing, refrigerate for 2 hours.

spread chocolate on bottom and sides of baking cups

STRAWBERRY ICE CREAM CAKE
(serves 10 to 12)

Angel Food Mix, 1 package
Flaked coconut, toasted, 1 cup
Kirsch, 2 tablespoons

Vanilla and strawberry ice cream, ½ gallon rectangular package

STRAWBERRY GLAZE

Frozen strawberries, 10-oz. package
Cornstarch, 1 tablespoon

Water, ¼ cup
Kirsch, 2 tablespoons
Red coloring, 5 drops

1. Follow directions for Angel Food Mix. Fold coconut and Kirsch into finished batter. Pour into 2 ungreased loaf pans (9" x 5" x 3"). Bake as directed. Cool. Remove from pans. Cut 1 loaf horizontally into 3 layers. (Freeze the other loaf unfilled.) Remove ice cream from package and cut in half the long way. Put cake together with layers of ice cream sandwiched in between. Freeze.

2. Purée strawberries in blender or through sieve. Bring to a boil in saucepan. Mix cornstarch with water and add to strawberries. Cook for 2 minutes. Cool. Add Kirsch and red coloring. Chill in freezer for 40 minutes, till thick. Spread on top and sides of cake. Refreeze. When firm, wrap in foil.

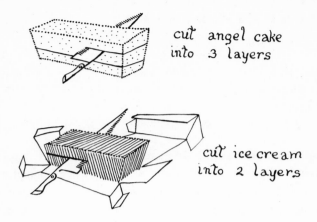

cut angel cake
into 3 layers

cut ice cream
into 2 layers

Serving day: Remove from freezer 20 minutes before serving. Serve with whipped cream and 2 thawed packages of frozen strawberries or raspberries.

CHOCOLATE ICE CREAM CAKE

(serves 10 or 12)

Follow directions for Strawberry Cake. Substitute rum for Kirsch, vanilla and chocolate ice cream for the vanilla and strawberry. Substitute Fudge Icing for Strawberry Glaze.

FUDGE ICING

Unsweetened chocolate, 4 ounces	Butter, 4 tablespoons
Sugar, 2 cups	Vanilla, 1 teaspoon
Cream, 1 cup	

Combine chocolate, sugar, and cream in saucepan. Stir over low heat until sugar is dissolved. Cook slowly without stirring to very soft-ball stage.* Add butter. Cool. Add vanilla and beat until thick. Spread on frozen cake and refreeze. When firm, wrap in foil.

See Note on Coffee Mousse recipe.

FROZEN ORANGE-CREAM CHOCOLATE DESSERT

(10 to 12 servings)

Heavy cream, 4 cups
Confectioner's sugar, sifted,
  1 cup
Orange juice, ¼ cup

Orange Curaçao, 4 tablespoons
Grated orange rind,
  2 tablespoons
Chocolate cooky crumbs, 1 cup

Whip cream until stiff. Fold in sugar, orange juice, Curaçao and grated rind. Place a layer of crumbs on bottom of refrigerator tray. Cover with layer of cream. Repeat the process of alternate thin layers and top with cream. Recipe will fill 2 refrigerator trays. Freeze and wrap.

Serving day: Unmold just before serving and cut into squares. Serve with Foamy Orange sauce.

unmold

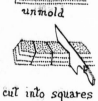

cut into squares

FOAMY ORANGE SAUCE

(1¼ cups)

Orange juice, ½ cup
Grated lemon rind, 1 teaspoon
Lemon juice, 1½ teaspoons
Sugar, 4 tablespoons

Eggs, separated, 2
Salt, ⅛ teaspoon
Orange Curaçao, 1 tablespoon
Mandarin oranges, 10-oz. can

Combine orange juice, lemon rind, lemon juice, sugar, and egg yolks in saucepan. Cook over low heat, stirring until thick. Cool. Whip egg whites and salt until thick. Gently fold into sauce. Stir in Curacao. Freeze.

Night before serving: Thaw in refrigerator for 24 hours. Before serving, stir in drained mandarin oranges.

PEARS IN WINE

Port wine, 1 cup
Water, ½ cup
Sugar, ½ cup
Lemon rind, ½ teaspoon
Cinnamon stick, 1" piece

Pears, 12 to 16
Apricot preserves, ¼ cup
Apricot brandy, 1 tablespoon
Red food coloring, few drops

Combine wine, water, sugar, lemon rind and cinnamon stick. Bring to a boil. Peel pears. Cut in half and remove core. Simmer a few at a time, until barely tender. Remove pears to freezer container. Add apricot preserves to syrup and cook until thickened. Add brandy and food coloring to syrup and pour over pears. Cool* and freeze.

Serving day: Thaw in refrigerator overnight or at room temperature for 5 to 6 hours. Serve as is, or combined with brandied black cherries.

Ready to serve without freezing.

STUFFED DATES
(about 32)

Dates, 8-oz. package
Cream cheese, 3 ounces
Sour cream, 1 tablespoon

Walnuts, chopped, 6 tablespoons
Granulated sugar, 2 tablespoons

Slit dates the long way, but not all the way through. Remove pits. Open to make a neat cavity. Blend cheese with sour cream and walnuts. Fill dates, mounding high. Roll bottoms in sugar.* Freeze on flat surface. Pack in container. (They will not stick to each other.) Freeze.

Serving day: Thaw at room temperature for 15 minutes. Serve, arranged on dessert plates with sliced fresh pineapple and canned guava shells.

To serve without freezing, refrigerate for 1 hour.

PUFF PASTE

Butter, 1 pound   Lemon juice, 2 tablespoons
Sifted flour, 4 cups   Ice water, 1⅓ cups
Salt, 1 teaspoon

1. Knead butter with your hands to free it of water and make it smooth and pliant. Reserve 4 tablespoons. Wrap remainder in foil and refrigerate.

2. Place flour in a large chilled bowl. Make a well in the center and put in the salt, lemon juice, 1 cup ice water and the 4 tablespoons butter. Using the finger tips, work center ingredients until smooth. Gradually work in the flour to form an elastic slightly sticky mass. If the dough seems too hard and dry, gradually work in the remaining ⅓ cup of water. Shape dough into a ball. Wrap in foil and a dish towel and refrigerate for 15 minutes.

3. On a floured board, using a chilled rolling pin, gently roll out dough into a long rectangle about ⅓" thick. Break off small pieces of the remaining chilled butter and arrange over the entire rectangle, leaving a 2" margin on all sides.

4. Fold dough in thirds from front to back, and then fold the left and right sides in towards the center, gently stretching if necessary. Seal edges and corners. Wrap in foil and a dish towel and refrigerate for 15 minutes. Chill rolling pin.

5. Place chilled dough on a floured board with one of the open ends facing you. Roll into a rectangle and fold in thirds from front to back. Wrap and chill for 15 minutes. Chill rolling pin.

6. Place dough again on floured board with open end towards you. Roll out and fold as before. Chill for 15 minutes. Chill rolling pin.

7. Again place dough on floured board with an open end towards you. Roll out into a long rectangle and fold in thirds from front to back. Turn folded dough so that open end is towards you and roll out again into a rectangle. Fold in thirds again from front to back. Wrap and chill for 30 minutes.

place
butter

fold in thirds   fold
                    up
                    sides

8. Repeat the entire operation, as described in the preceding paragraph, one more time. Wrap in foil and refrigerate for a minimum of 3 hours before using. (The dough can be kept in the refrigerator for 2 or 3 days but it cannot be frozen until it has been shaped.)

Note: Do your rolling and turning in a cool place, like a cool basement or near an open window, so that the butter does not soften and break through the paste. Also keep your rolling pin in the freezer between turns. Don't try puff paste in warm weather.

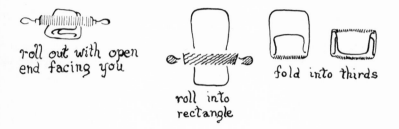

roll out with open end facing you

roll into rectangle

fold into thirds

CROUSTADES
(about 48)

Puff Paste, 1 recipe

1. Roll out paste about ¼" thick. Cut into rectangles 2" x 3". Brush with egg yolk beaten with a little water.* Place in freezer on a flat pan. When frozen, pack in container and freeze.

Serving day: Place frozen rectangle on a baking sheet lined with ungreased brown paper. Bake at 400° F. for 15 to 20 minutes. Cool on rack. To serve, slit tops off with a sharp knife, fill cavity and replace tops.

> *To serve without freezing, refrigerate for 30 minutes. Bake as directed.

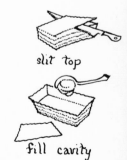

slit top

fill cavity

PATTY SHELLS

(about 16)

Puff Paste, 1 recipe

1. Roll out puff paste ⅛" thick. Cut into 3" rounds.

cut
3-inch rounds

2. In half the rounds, cut out 2" centers, leave ½" rings. Moisten the edges of each 3" round and place one ring on each. Place patty shells and centers on a flat surface and put in freezer for 30 minutes.

cut out centers
from half the
rounds

3. When firm, gently brush the rings and 2" centers with egg yolk diluted with water. Lay the centers lightly inside the rings.* Replace in freezer on flat pan. When firm, pack in container and freeze.

place rings on
rounds

Serving day: Place shells on baking sheet covered with ungreased brown paper. Bake at 400° F. for 10 minutes. Reduce heat to 350° F. and bake for 15 minutes. Remove centers and put shells and tops back at 350° F. for 5 more minutes to dry inside. Cool on rack. Just before serving, fill with Lobster Béchamel or other fillings and replace tops.

> *To serve without freezing, refrigerate for 30 minutes. Bake as directed.

PUFF PASTE STARS

(about 48)

Puff Paste, 1 recipe (see index)   Apricot preserves, 1 cup
Egg white, 1   (or any thick jam)

1. Roll out paste ¼" thick. Cut into 3" squares. Make 4 cuts, 1½" long, from the corners toward the center. Place ½ teaspoon of jam in the center.

2. Beat an egg white with a teaspoon of water. Dip your thumb and forefinger into it and fold 4 corners (every other one) back to the center over the jam, pressing together with your egged-fingers. The shape will be a swirled 4-pointed star.* Place on flat

cut from   fold alternate
corners   corners to
to center   center

surface and freeze. When firm, pack in container and return to freezer.

Serving day: Place stars on baking sheet covered with ungreased brown paper. Bake at 400° F. for 10 minutes. Reduce heat to 275° F. and bake another 15 minutes.

> **To serve without freezing, refrigerate for 30 minutes. Bake as directed.*

PUFF PASTE MIRLITONS
(32)

Puff Paste, 1 recipe (see index)
Eggs, at room temperature, 6
Sugar, 1½ cups
Vanilla, ½ teaspoon

Finely crushed dry macaroons, 1½ cups
Apricot jam, ⅓ cup
Almonds, blanched, shelled and halved, ½ cup

1. Roll out puff paste on a floured board. Cut into 3½" or 4" rounds and line muffin tins or tart shells. Prick bottoms with a fork and place in a freezer while you make the filling.

2. Beat eggs with sugar over hot water until thickened and lemon colored. Remove from heat and add vanilla and crushed macaroons. Cool.

3. Place ½ teaspoon apricot jam in each tart. Add egg mixture and top with a few almond halves.* Freeze on flat pan in freezer. When frozen, pack carefully in container and replace in freezer.

Serving day: Replace frozen tarts in original muffin tins or tart shells. While still frozen, place in 450° F. oven and bake for 10 minutes. Reduce heat to 300° F. and bake for 25 to 30 minutes until filling is set.

Note: To dry macaroons, break into small pieces, spread out on a baking pan and set in a 200° F. oven for 30 minutes. Cool on pan.

> **To serve without freezing, refrigerate for 30 minutes. Bake as directed.*

apricot jam

line muffin tins
with pastry rounds

CURRANT-FILLED TURNOVERS
(about 45)

Currants, 1 cup
Rum, 3 tablespoons
Ground lemon peel,
  2 tablespoons

Brown sugar, ¼ cup
Butter, 4 tablespoons
Puff Paste, 1 recipe (see index)

1. Wash currants and let soak in rum for 45 minutes to an hour. Combine currants, lemon peel, sugar and butter in a small pan. Cook over low heat for about 10 minutes, stirring occasionally. Cool.

2. Roll out puff paste, about ⅛″ thick, on lightly floured board. Cut into 3″ squares. Put a teaspoon of filling in each square. Moisten edges with cold water, fold over corners to make a triangle and seal edges by pressing together with tongs of a fork. Brush top with egg yolk beaten with a little water.* Freeze on flat surface. Pack in containers when firm. Return to freezer.

Serving day: Place frozen turnovers on baking sheet covered with ungreased brown paper. Bake at 400° F. for 18 to 20 minutes.

Note: You can use marmalade or fruit jam or preserves for the filling if preferred.

    *To serve without freezing, refrigerate for 30 minutes. Bake as directed.

cut into square   fold into triangle

EXTRA NOTES ABOUT DESSERTS

Cake should be frozen after baking but cookies can be frozen unbaked or baked. Pie pastry is better frozen before baking. Bake filled pies, unthawed, on lowest shelf of oven. Apple sauce and fruit purées freeze well. Thaw for 6 hours at room temperature or overnight in the refrigerator.

stockpiling
and garnishes

10

In the wonderful world which your freezer makes possible, don't overlook the advantages of stock-piling, that is, of building up an inventory during idle hours to fill the demand for busier days.

On a rainy day, spend a few hours shelling nuts, grating cheese, cooking stock or toasting croutons; chop several pounds of green peppers, or sauté a few pounds of mushrooms to have on hand. And always when chopping onions, chop a few more for the freezer, or make a brown sauce in sufficient quantity to freeze part of it.

Don't neglect to freeze foods which are perishable or seasonal. You'll find suggestions in the pages which follow. A few tricks with leftovers and decorative garnishes are also included.

BUTTER

FREEZING BUTTER

Wrap in foil or freezer paper and freeze. Will keep for months. You'll never run out of a slice of butter for that "royal slice of bread." To use: Thaw in refrigerator for about 3 hours or at room temperature for 1 to 2 hours.

BUTTER BALLS

dip in hot water

Dip a melon-ball cutter in hot water and scoop butter balls out of a 1-pound brick package. Drop in ice water as you scoop. Remove from ice water, place on a flat surface and freeze. When firm, pack in container or bag and store in freezer. To use: Serve, piled in a decorative pyramid on a butter dish or on individual butter plates. They thaw in 10 to 15 minutes.

scoop out balls

drop in ice water

HERB BUTTER

Butter, ¼ pound   Chives, minced, 1 tablespoon
Parsley, minced, 1 tablespoon

Melt butter. Mix in herbs. Cool and freeze. To use: Stir into cooked drained vegetables, or spread on cocktail bread slices or rye bread and serve.

GARLIC BUTTER

Combine ¼ pound butter and 2 minced cloves of garlic. Follow same procedure as with Herb Butter.

CHEESE

GRATED CHEESE

Grate and pack in container. To use: Use directly from the freezer in cooking or to sprinkle on soups, pastas, or au gratin dishes. Stir into sauces. It is useful to have Swiss cheese, already grated, to add to any dish. Buy the finest Parmesan cheese in one piece, grate it, and keep it in the freezer. Much better than commercially grated varieties.

BLEU CHEESE OR ROQUEFORT

Wrap in foil and freeze. To use: Thaw at room temperature. After freezing it is more crumbly than fresh cheese, and perfect for sprinkling on salads or mixing in salad dressing.

CREAM

Left-over cream, if still very fresh, can be frozen in freezer containers. To use: Light creams may be used for cooking only, directly from freezer or thawed. Not for table use. Use heavy cream for whipping, after thawing in refrigerator.

WHIPPED CREAM MOUNDS

Whip heavy cream, sweetened or unsweetened, and arrange in mounds on a cooky sheet. (Use a pastry bag or a spoon to shape into neat cones.) Freeze on sheet. When frozen, pack in container. Mounds will not stick together. To use: Thaw at room temperature for 5 to 10 minutes. Use as decorative toppings for pies, cakes, ice cream or soups. Very pretty and convenient.

SAUTEED GARLIC CROUTONS

White bread, 1 unsliced loaf   Garlic, crushed, 3 cloves
Butter, ½ pound

Remove crusts from bread and cut it into ½ inch cubes. Dry cubes in 300° F. oven for 2 or 3 minutes. Heat butter and garlic in skillet. Sauté bread cubes until golden brown, turning to brown all sides. Drain on absorbent paper.* Pack in plastic bag or container. Freeze.

Serving day: Heat in 300° F. oven for 5 or 10 minutes, until warm. Serve in soup or sprinkled on vegetables.

    Ready to serve without freezing.

CROUTONS

Cut stale bread into cubes. Toast in oven with or without melted butter. Freeze in bag or container. To use: Thaw at room temperature for 5 minutes. Use as garnish in soup or stir into cooked vegetables.

remove crusts
from bread

BREAD CRUMBS

Stale bread makes wonderful crumbs in any size you want. Freeze in bag or container. Label quantity. Use directly from freezer, for breading foods, for *au gratin* dishes or for stuffing.

BUTTERED CRUMBS

Mix melted butter with crumbs. Pack in container and freeze. Use directly from freezer for casserole topping.

CAKE AND COOKY CRUMBS

Crumble leftover cake or cookies and place in container in freezer. Use directly from freezer and sprinkle on ice cream or puddings.

CANAPES

Bread canapés, which require heating or toasting before serving, freeze well; but open-face canapés dry out quickly after thawing at room temperature. It is better to freeze your favorite fillings and make the canapés the day of the party.

EGGS

HARD-COOKED EGG YOLKS, GRATED

Grate yolks and freeze in ice cube trays. Package in bags. Defrost and use for decorating canapés, vegetables, salads, etc.

EGG YOLKS

Beat lightly with a fork. Stir in 1 teaspoon of salt or 1 tablespoon sugar to each cup of yolks. Freeze in small container or ice cube tray. (Eject cubes when frozen and store in a plastic bag.) Label as to quantity of yolks, salt and sugar. (About 14 egg yolks equals 1 cup.) To use: Thaw at room temperature or in refrigerator. Use as soon as thawed.

EGG WHITES

Do not mix. Pack in small container or ice cube tray. Label quantity and freeze. (8 egg whites equals 1 cup.) To use: Thaw at room temperature or in refrigerator before beating. Will keep in refrigerator for a day or two.

POULTRY GIBLETS

Keep a half gallon container in your freezer for storing poultry giblets. Every time you cook a chicken, store the giblets there until the container is full. Store no longer than 3 months. To use: Make a delicious soup from giblets alone or add them to the soup you're making from a fowl to make it even richer, or eat the giblets for dinner with a cream sauce made with chicken stock and serve with rice.

CHICKEN LIVERS

Keep a separate container in the freezer to store livers and raw chicken fat accumulated from each chicken you cook. Store no longer than 3 months. To use: Thaw slightly, enough to slice. Sauté the fat and liver combined with sliced onions. Chop for chopped liver.

slice meat

THINLY SLICED STEAKS OR POULTRY BREASTS

Remove bones from raw meat and poultry. Freeze for one hour. This makes slicing easy. A good trick when preparing Chinese dishes, such as Beef with Peppers or Chow Mein.

GRAVY

Freeze leftover gravy in small containers or ice cube trays. Eject cubes when frozen and store in plastic bag. Label quantity. Also use freezer to quickly chill gravy, soup, stews, etc. until fat congeals for easy removal.

To use: Heat directly from the freezer or thaw to enrich sauces or sliced meat.

CHICKEN, VEAL OR BEEF BROTH

Freeze in ice cube trays. When frozen, eject cubes and store in a plastic bag in freezer. (8 cubes equals 1 cup.)
To use: Heat directly from the freezer or thaw. Add to cooked dishes, gravys, soups, sauces etc.

eject cubes....
pack in bag

EXTRA NOTES
ABOUT VEGETABLES

To freeze potato pancakes, fry only until golden, freeze, and finish frying before serving.

Baked stuffed potatoes can be frozen and reheated with the skin wrapped in foil, in 350° F. oven for 1 hour.

Mashed white or sweet potatoes can be frozen in patties and reheated by browning in butter.

Baked beans freeze well. Reheat, covered, at 350° F. until piping hot.

Freeze vegetable purées to combine with chicken or beef stock and cream, if you like, to create unusual soups.

CHINESE NOODLES

Buy them by the pound in a Chinese market or from your neighborhood Chinese restaurant. They are much better than canned and will keep for months in the freezer. Use directly from freezer or heat slightly in a low oven.

FISHERMAN'S CATCH

If there is a fisherman in your family and he catches more than you can eat, you either give it away or freeze it.

To freeze: Clean thoroughly and leave whole, cut in steaks or in fillets. Lean fish should be dipped into a solution of ¼ cup salt to 1 quart cold water for 20 seconds. Wrap in freezer paper, separating fillets or steaks by 2 layers of paper.

Whole fish can be frozen in an ice block to keep it from drying out. Place the fish in a container or pan to fit it, cover with cold water and freeze. When frozen, remove block from pan and wrap in foil or freezer paper. Return to freezer. Do not keep fish in freezer longer than 6 weeks.

To use: Cook directly from the freezer, allowing extra cooking time. If necessary to thaw, put it in refrigerator.

wrap ice block in foil

cover fish with cold water

MUSHROOMS

SLICED SAUTEED MUSHROOMS

Mushrooms, sliced, 4 cups   Butter, 4 tablespoons
  (1 pound)

Melt butter in skillet and cook mushrooms for 5 minutes, stirring occasionally. Cool. Package in small, covered jelly jars or ½ pint containers. Freeze. To use: Thaw for ½ hour. Stir into cooked drained vegetables, or rice, or noodles, and heat through. Heat and pour over broiled steak.

broil, cup
side up

BROILED MUSHROOM CAPS

Brush with melted butter and broil for 2 minutes, cup side up. Freeze. To use: Thaw for 10 minutes and finish broiling at low heat.

RAW MUSHROOMS

It is possible to freeze mushrooms raw for 2 or 3 weeks. Freeze only perfect ones and as soon as you bring them home. Do not wash, clean or cut them. Pack in absolutely air-tight container. Use *without* thawing. (Sautéing or broiling is a better method of freezing mushrooms because the raw ones may get rubbery.)

GREEN PEPPERS

Wash and cut off stems. Cut in half and remove seeds. Slice, chop or cut in rings. Spread out in a single layer on a flat surface and freeze. When frozen, pack in container. Label quantity and freeze. Use thawed or frozen in cooking. Use raw in salads such as aspics where a slight loss of crispness is not noticeable. Stock up when they are in season and you always have some handy to dress up any dish or leftover.

chop, slice or cut in rings

CHOPPED ONIONS OR SHALLOTS

Chop coarsely. Spread out in a single layer on a flat surface and freeze immediately before juice forms. When frozen, break up with a fork and pack in small container. Label quantity and freeze. Use in cooking without thawing. Very convenient to have onions already chopped whenever you want them. Also, shallots aren't always available in all markets. When you buy a basket, plan to chop and freeze part of it.

LEMONS

Grated Rind

Pack in small plastic bag or foil and label quantity. Place bag in container and freeze. Use thawed or frozen in cooking, baking or as a garnish.

Juice

Pack in an ice cube tray and freeze. When frozen, pop out frozen lemon juice and pack in plastic bag or container. Each cube will hold juice of 1 lemon. To use: Thaw and use in pastry making or cakes. Add while frozen to hot sauces. So convenient to have when there isn't a fresh lemon in the house.

HERBS

Freezing is a good way to preserve your summer garden herbs for use during the whole year. I freeze basil, mint, parsley and tarragon. They have a fresher, better flavor than the dried herbs. Wash and dry thoroughly. Discard stems. Pack in small bags and place in freezer container. Freeze. To use: Chop while still frozen and use without thawing. Good only for cooking, because crispness is lost in freezing.

pack herbs in bags

place bags in container

RAW CRANBERRIES

Good to freeze because they are easy to prepare for freezing and because their season is short. No blanching needed. Wash, drain, pack in containers, leaving room at the top. Freeze. Use directly from the freezer. Grind into relish or cook into sauce. Add to a ham while it's baking, or to Sauerbraten, pot roast or braised duck as they cook.

CRANBERRY CREAM
(3 pints)

Raw cranberries, 4 cups   Sugar, 1 cup
Onion, 2 medium   Horseradish, 5 tablespoons
Sour cream, 1½ cups

Put cranberries and onions through food grinder. Stir in sour cream, sugar and horseradish. Pack in small containers. Freeze.

Serving day: Thaw in refrigerator overnight or thaw at room temperature for 4 or 5 hours.

CRANBERRY PIE GARNISH
(12 rounds)

Flour, sifted, 1 cup   Egg white, 1
Salt, ½ teaspoon   Cranberry-Orange Relish, 1 cup
Shortening, ⅓ cup   (see index for recipe)
Ice water, 2 tablespoons

1. Combine flour and salt and sift again. Cut in shortening until particles are the size of coarse corn meal. Sprinkle on water a little at a time. With a fork, press moistened particles together until dough holds together. Turn out on wax paper and form into a ball. Chill in refrigerator for 30 minutes.

2. Roll out ⅛" thick. Cut into 3" rounds. Brush edges with beaten egg white. Cut scraps into narrow strips. Curve and place them around the edge of the round as a rim. With your fingers,

place strips on rounds
in a rim .... press firmly

press them firmly to each other and to the bottom. Freeze on a flat surface. Pack in container, layered if necessary. (No separating paper is needed.) Freeze.

fill with relish

Serving day: Place rounds on an ungreased baking sheet and prick bottoms with a fork. Bake on an upper shelf at 450° F. for 8 to 10 minutes until lightly browned. When cool, fill with a heaping mound of cranberry relish. Use to garnish roasted poultry, lamb, or pork.

CRANBERRY-ORANGE RELISH
(about 3 pints)

Raw cranberries, 4 cups   Sugar, 1¼ cups
Oranges, rind and pulp, 2

Put cranberries and oranges through food grinder, using coarse opening. Mix with sugar. Pack in container. Freeze.

Serving day: Thaw in refrigerator overnight or thaw at room temperature for 4 or 5 hours.

FROZEN HORSE-RADISH SHERBET
(about 1½ cups)

Heavy cream, ½ cup   Sugar, 1 teaspoon
Grated fresh horse-radish, ½ cup   Salt, ½ teaspoon
Orange juice, 2 tablespoons

Whip cream until stiff. Fold in other ingredients. Pack in container. Freeze.

Serving day: Defrost at room temperature for about 30 minutes. Break up and stir with a fork or spoon. The texture should be icy, not creamy. Serve in a bowl to accompany fish, boiled beef, tongue or ham, etc.

SAUCES

BROWN SAUCE

(1 quart)

Meat or bacon drippings, ½ cup
Onion, coarsely chopped, 2
Carrot, chopped, 1
Celery, chopped, 1 stalk
Flour, ½ cup
Beef broth, 8 cups
Tomato paste, 1 teaspoon

Parsley, 4 sprigs
Bay leaf, 1
Garlic, crushed, 1 clove
Thyme, pinch
Peppercorns, 4
Salt, 1 teaspoon

press through sieve

Heat drippings in a heavy pot and sauté onion, carrot, and celery over low heat for 10 minutes, stirring occasionally. Blend in flour and cook for about 10 minutes over moderate heat, stirring until flour and vegetables are golden brown. Gradually add 4 cups of broth, stirring to scrape up browned flour, and cook until thick and smooth. Add remaining broth and other ingredients. Cover and simmer for 2 to 2½ hours until reduced in half. Strain through a fine sieve, pressing through juice of vegetables. Chill. Remove fat which has risen to the top. Pour into 1 or 2 cup freezer containers and freeze. When frozen, you may remove contents and wrap in foil or plastic bags.

Serving day: Heat and use as a base for many sauces.

MADEIRA SAUCE: Add ⅓ cup of Madeira and 1 tablespoon of butter.

MUSHROOM SAUCE: Add ⅓ cup sautéed mushrooms and 1 tablespoon sautéed shallots.

MUSTARD SAUCE: Add ½ cup white wine and 2 tablespoons Dijon mustard creamed with 2 teaspoons butter.

RED WINE SAUCE: Add 2 tablespoons sautéed shallots and ⅓ cup red wine.

CHICKEN-LIVER SAUCE: Add 3 chicken livers, simmered in stock until tender, drained and puréed, and 2 tablespoons currant jelly to 2 cups brown sauce.

HOLLANDAISE SAUCE
(2 cups)

Butter, ½ pound
Egg yolks, 8
Lemon juice, 2 tablespoons

Salt, ½ teaspoon
Cream, 2 tablespoons

Melt butter in the top of double boiler over hot water. Remove from heat. Using a wire whisk, gradually beat in egg yolks, lemon juice and salt. Beat well. Place again over hot, not boiling water. Stir well for about 5 minutes until the sauce thickens. Stir in cream and remove from heat. Cool. Pack in container. Freeze.

Serving day: Heat in top of double boiler over hot water, stirring until thickened.

pour boiling water on grated coconut

COCONUT

GRATED

Grate and freeze in small container. Thaw for 15 minutes at room temperature and stir into cooked, drained vegetables or sprinkle on fruit or ice cream.

TOASTED GRATED

Spread grated coconut on baking sheet and brown lightly in moderate oven for about 10 minutes. Freeze in small container. Sprinkle, directly from freezer, on vegetables or desserts.

COCONUT MILK

Pour boiling water on grated coconut and steep for 30 minutes. Strain and pour milk into container. Use in cooking.

NUTS

ALMONDS

Blanched: Blanch almonds by placing them in boiling water for 2 minutes. Drain and slip off skins.

Chopped: Chop after blanching.

Ground: Grind in blender after blanching.

Toasted slivered: Slice blanched almonds while still warm. Spread on a shallow pan and stir in melted butter (2 tablespoons butter to 1 cup of almonds). Toast in 325° F. oven for 20 minutes, stirring occasionally, until lightly browned. Or brown with butter in a skillet over low heat, stirring occasionally.

Chopped Toasted: Toast whole blanched almonds in oven and chop. Freeze any of above in small containers. To use: Use directly from freezer. Stir into vegetable or meat dishes. Sprinkle on top of casseroles or soups. Use in pastry, cookies or cakes.

TOASTED BRAZIL NUTS

Place in plastic bag and freeze for 24 hours or longer. Crack and remove shells from frozen nuts. Slice thinly and toast in 350° F. oven for about 12 to 15 minutes. Pack in container and freeze. Use directly from freezer in baking. Or mix with cranberry relish or in fruit pies.

CHESTNUTS

peel chestnuts

Cover chestnuts with boiling water and simmer for 2 or 3 minutes. While hot, remove shells and skins. Slice, chop or leave whole. Freeze in small bag or container. To use: Use frozen or thawed in many ways. Brown in butter and mix with vegetables. Simmer in chicken broth and purée as a vegetable. Stir into poultry or meat dishes or use in stuffings. Boil and mix with a sweet syrup and mix with fruit or purée with a sweet syrup and pour over ice cream.

PECANS OR WALNUTS

Freeze whole or chopped and pack in small container. Use frozen or thawed. Invaluable in baking.

PISTACHIO NUTS

Roast in 350° F. oven for 15 to 20 minutes. Then rub off skins. Chop and freeze. To use, sprinkle on desserts.

ICE BLOCKS, CUBES, ETC.

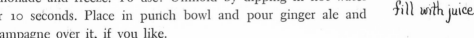

pour in juice half-way

FRUIT JUICE ICE BLOCK

Combine frozen fruit juices, such as orange and pineapple, lemonade and grape juice. Freeze in any container. To use: Unmold and place in punch bowl.

place fruit on frozen layer

FRUIT JUICE ICE RING

Prepare frozen pineapple-orange juice as directed on can. Pour into ring mold, halfway up, and freeze. Place orange and lemon slices on top of frozen layer. Fill the rest of ring with prepared lemonade and freeze. To use: Unmold by dipping in hot water for 10 seconds. Place in punch bowl and pour ginger ale and champagne over it, if you like.

fill with juice

EXTRA ICE CUBES

Make ahead of the party and store in plastic bags. (Work quickly so that they won't melt and stick together.)

COFFEE OR TEA ICE CUBES

Freeze regular strength coffee in ice cube trays. To use: Fill tall glasses with the cubes and pour regular strength hot coffee over them for iced coffee. Tea, same procedure.

DECORATIVE ICE BOWL

half-fill bowl
with water

tape 2 bowls
together

arrange flowers

2 nested bowls, one 2"-3" less in
diameter than the other

Choice of:
Artificial flowers or leaves
Fresh flowers or leaves
Orange, lemon or lime slices
Strawberries
Clusters of grapes

1. Fill largest bowl half full of cold water. Place in it the smaller bowl, centering by taping the 2 bowls together in 4 places with freezer tape. Arrange decorative materials in the circle of water around the inner bowl. Place in freezer.

2. When water is partially frozen, arrange another circle of decoration on top of ice, using the same materials. Pour in water to the top and return to freezer.

3. When frozen, remove from freezer. Remove tapes and pour hot water into inner bowl. Let stand a few minutes until bowl can be removed from ice. Set outer bowl in hot water for a few seconds until ice bowl is released. Place on a sheet of foil and return to freezer until ready to use.

Serving day: Place ice bowl on a serving platter with an edge or a hollow to catch any drippings. It will keep well for about 3 hours.

Suggested Uses:

1. As a centerpiece filled with fresh strawberries, surrounded by mint leaves and clusters of grapes. Serve for dessert, perhaps with cheese cake or lemon dessert.

2. Fill with love apples (tiny tomatoes) and cucumber sticks. Or with radish roses and raw finocchio sticks. Serve as a salad.

3. Fill with ice cream balls which will keep for 1 hour at room temperature in ice bowl. Scoop ice cream into balls and place on a flat surface, freezing until firm before placing in the bowl. Surround with bowls of sauces, whipped cream and nuts.

4. Fill with a flower arrangement, harmonizing the colors and the decorations in the ice bowl. For example, in an ice bowl decorated with orange or lemon slices, arrange daffodils and baby's breath; or arrange deep pink roses in a bowl of light pink rosebuds.

THINGS TO DO WITH ICE CREAM

ICE CREAM BALLS

A few hours before your party, shape ice cream into balls with a scoop. Freeze quickly on a flat tray. When firm, arrange different flavors in a glass bowl and store in freezer. To use: Remove from freezer 10 to 15 minutes before serving.

COCONUT SNOW BALLS

Roll ice cream balls in shredded or flaked coconut. Freeze on flat surface. When frozen, wrap each ball in foil. To use: Unwrap and serve in glass dishes with crème de menthe or chocolate sauce.

PARFAITS

Fill parfait glasses with alternate layers of ice cream and sauce, top with whipped cream and place in freezer. Try chocolate ice cream with marshmallow sauce. Vanilla ice cream goes well with a sauce made from crushing canned brandied peaches, or with a raspberry sauce made by thawing frozen raspberries and puréeing them in the blender.

To use: Thaw at room temperature for 15 minutes.

Your Own Flavor of Ice Cream

Take commercial ice cream, place in a chilled bowl and let soften slightly. Using a fork or slotted spoon, mix flavoring through ice cream until somewhat blended, but do not let ice cream melt. Pack in container and freeze. To use: Scoop out and eat.

Try these: Vanilla ice cream with banana purée or frozen fruit, thawed and puréed; chocolate ice cream, with crème de menthe or chopped pistachio nuts; strawberry ice cream with Kirsch liquor; or coffee ice cream with shaved chocolate.

COCKTAIL TIDBITS, LEFTOVERS AND ODDMENTS

When you use only a part of a can or jar of pickles, olives, pimientos, cocktail onions, water chestnuts, chocolate sprinkles, or tomato paste, freeze the rest, before they spoil, in a plastic container. Original jar can be used if glass or plastic. Use directly from freezer or thawed.

PRETZELS, POTATO CHIPS AND OTHER COCKTAIL TIDBITS

Pack cellophane bags inside plastic bag. (Do not keep longer than 1 month.) Before using, thaw at room temperature or heat slightly in low oven.

GLASSES AND PLATES

dip glasses
into lemon juice

Chill cocktail glasses, salad and dessert plates in freezer for 15 to 20 minutes before serving. Use when serving cold foods or drinks.

FROSTED GLASSES

dip into
sugar

Dip the rims of glasses into lemon juice about ½ inch deep and then into very fine or confectioners' sugar. Place in freezer for 15 to 20 minutes. Use for Whiskey Sours, Daiquiris, Tom Collins, Planters Punch or iced tea. Punch cups also frost prettily.

COFFEE

If you like a particular type of coffee which you can only find in some distant store, buy it ground to order and keep fresh flavor by freezing in 1 pound coffee cans. Use directly from the freezer.

SHAVED OR CHOPPED CHOCOLATE

Pack in container. Freeze. Use directly from freezer, as a garnish for desserts.

MARSHMALLOWS

Freeze in plastic bag. To use, cut with scissors while still frozen and use in sauces and desserts or as a garnish for ice cream. Never dries up.

party menus

Late Supper
Chocolate-Date Cake
Coffee

Cocktail Buffet
Lobster Bechamel

Greek Dinner
Lamb Avgolemono

Italian Dinner
Petti di Pollo Lombardy

Luncheon
Gazpacho soup

Indian Dinner
Lamb Curry

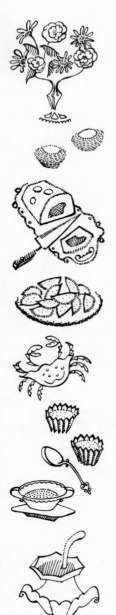

Composing a meal is like painting a picture. You start with a center of interest and build around it. Choose the entree first. Then plan the rest of the meal to contrast or complement in texture, flavor and color.

If the pièce de résistance is meat with a sauce, consider a pasta or starch dish to absorb the sauce, Then, vary the texture with a crisp vegetable or a vegetable with crisp additions to it. If your main dish is chewy and crisp, a sauced or soft vegetable goes well.

A spicy, tomato-flavored entree calls for a bland accompaniment. A hot, highly seasoned dish retains its taste enjoyment best with the contrast of sweetly touched side dishes.

Think of color, too. If your entree has a cream-colored sauce, and you want to serve rice with it, mix the cooked rice with parsley and melted butter and bake it to a lovely green tint. For a bright note of color, try grilled tomatoes, pimiento, or sautéed red peppers.

The hors d'oeuvres might feature one hot dish, and one or two cold spreads, dips, or canapes, as well as nibble foods like olives, radishes, raw vegetable sticks and nuts. When the entree is meat, a sea food or cheese dish is a natural preface. With a poultry dish try barbecued meat balls or liver turnovers.

Now what about dessert? This depends on the main dish—its richness and flavor. After a highly seasoned entree, a tart lemon or refreshing pineapple dessert is welcome. A light-textured, delicately seasoned chicken suggests a sweet, rich strawberry or chocolate concoction.

A few sample menus follow. Mostly these are of dishes which can be cooked and frozen. Not every food can be. So I've rounded out the menus with other dishes to be cooked on *the* day—or the day before. The freezable dishes are marked with an asterisk and you'll find those recipes in the book.

DINNER

*Hot Cheese Turnovers
*Lobster Chunks with Sour Cream Dip
Cucumber Sticks with Russian Dressing   Olives, Radishes
*Hungarian Goulash   *Polenta   Onion Rye Bread (bought)
Salad of Cooked Peas, Tiny Canned Beets   Sour Cream dressing:
(½ cup sour cream mixed with 3 tablespoons tar-
ragon wine vinegar, 1 tablespoon chopped chives,
salt and paprika.)
*Strawberry Lady Finger Cake   Coffee

DINNER

*Lobster Americaine   *Pâté with Cognac with sesame crackers
*Poulet à La Vallée D'Auge   *Barley Pilaf
Cooked String Beans with *Toasted Sliced Almonds
French Bread
Endive, sliced tomato, and chopped basil with oil and vinegar
*Croquembouche   Coffee

DINNER

*Hot Pastry Turnovers filled with chopped meat
*Hot Mushroom Hors D'oeuvres
*Marinated Green Peppers with anchovies
*Bouillabaisse
*Flageolet Salad:
Served on Boston lettuce with slivers of endive,
prosciutto ham and zucchini à la grecque.
*Cheese Cake
Served with fresh strawberries steeped in Kirsch.
Espresso Coffee with cinnamon sticks

DINNER

Cucumber Boats filled with cream cheese blended
with chopped smoked salmon and sour cream
*Onion Soup with toasted French bread
*Stuffed Chicken Breasts in Pastry Crust
*Broccoli Mold   Lentil Salad:
Prepared in same manner as flageolet Salad (See
index). Serve on endive.
*Parfait Colettes   Coffee

DINNER

*Quenelles de Poisson aux Sauce Cardinal
Cold Celeri Remoulade:
Shredded raw celery knob mixed with mayonnaise,
Dijon mustard and tarragon vinegar and sprinkled
with chopped chives.
*Gigot en Croûte
*Zucchini stuffed with pea purée
*Flageolet Salad arranged on lettuce
*Apricot Meringue Torte   Coffee and Tea

DINNER

*Cheese Straws   *Lobster Americaine
*Tipsy Duck   *Chestnut Purée in Orange Shells
Marinated Asparagus Salad:
Cooked and chilled asparagus, mixed with French
dressing and Dijon mustard. Serve on lettuce and
sprinkle with crumbled, hard-cooked egg yolk and
chopped chives.
*Garlic Bread
*Apple Charlotte   Coffee and Tea

DINNER

*Hot Cheese Turnovers
*Soupe de Poissons Mediterranée
*Petti di Pollo Lombardy
*Stuffed Mushrooms Florentine   *Herb-Spiral Bread
Green salad garnished with sliced canned hearts of palm
and pitted black olives
*Chocolate-Coffee Bombe   Espresso

DINNER

*Quiche Lorraine
Eggplant Caviar:
Bake a whole eggplant at 350° F. till soft. Peel and
chop finely with 2 onions, 4 garlic cloves, and 4
peeled tomatoes. Add ½ cup olive oil, salt and
pepper and chill overnight in refrigerator. Serve very
cold with cocktail rye bread.
*Boeuf Bourguignon   *Pignole Pilaf
Fresh or frozen asparagus with *Hollandaise Sauce
*Onion Bread
Raw Spinach Salad, with red onion rings sprinkled
with crumbled hard-cooked egg yolk.
*Chocolate Mousse and Pistachio Ice Cream Bombe
* Cherry Crescents   Coffee

ITALIAN DINNER

*Shrimp Marinara
Italian Salami and Melon slices   Cherry Tomatoes
*Italian Veal Rolls   *Risotto alla Milanese
Cold Zucchini à la Grecque served on lettuce
Italian Bread Sticks
*Orange-Cream Chocolate Dessert   Espresso with lemon peel

GREEK DINNER

*Spanakopetes
Eggplant Caviar (see index for recipe)
*Lamb with Zucchini, Avgolemono
Rice Pilaf with chick peas:

Sauté raw rice in butter until golden. Add chicken stock and cook until tender. Sauté chopped onion and drained chick peas in oil for 5 minutes. Add drained pea liquid and lemon juice and cook for 10 minutes. Mix into rice.

Green salad:

Garnished with chilled green beans, cooked and marinated in oil, lemon juice, salt, pepper and crushed garlic. Serve cold sprinkled with Feta cheese.

Greek bread from bakery
*Pears in wine
Assorted cheeses and fine crackers
Coffee or Espresso served with cinnamon stick

CHINESE DINNER

*Fried Shrimp Balls with Spicy Sauce
Fish Ball and Watercress Soup

Heat 2½ quarts of chicken broth (from the freezer). Add 1 teaspoon salt, ¼ teaspoon white pepper, ¼ cup sherry, 3 bunches watercress with stems removed, 1 bunch chopped scallions and 1 can of whole bamboo shoots, sliced, and cook for 5 minutes. Add 2 cups canned fish balls to soup and serve hot.

Roast Duck, basted with sauce
(½ cup honey, ½ cup boiling water, ¼ cup soy sauce and 2 crushed garlic cloves.)
*Sweet and Sour Pork   *Fried Rice
*Stuffed Dates served with fresh pineapple chunks
and canned guava shells
Chinese Tea

CURRY DINNER

*Devilled Crab
Raw Cauliflowerets with Russian Dressing
Carrot curls   Olives

Prepare raw vegetables in morning, crisp in ice water
in refrigerator.

*Indian Lamb Curry
White Rice

Cook rice until tender. Place in a colander and pour
boiling water through it to remove starch. Let drain
thoroughly. (This much can be done in the morning.) Place in buttered casserole, cover and reheat
in slow oven for about an hour.

Thinly Sliced Preserved Kumquats and Diced Avocado
in Lemon-Jello Mold

Substitute ¼ cup of kumquat syrup for part of the
2 cups of water required with 1 package of Jello. Use
1 cup of sliced kumquats and 2 avocados. (Makes
1 quart.) Make in morning or the day before.

Diced Cucumbers and Chopped Red Onion, mixed with yogurt
or sour cream, toasted cumin seed and salt and pepper to taste

Remove peel and seeds from cucumber before dicing.
For 3 cucumbers use 1 cup of cream. Make in
morning or the day before.

*Grated Fresh Coconut Toasted   Chutney (commercial)
*Sliced Toasted Almonds
*Herb Bread
Green Salad with Artichokes à la Grecque

Cook frozen artichokes in combination of 1 cup of
water, ½ cup olive oil, 2 tablespoons white wine and
1 tablespoon lemon juice; seasoned with ½ teaspoon
salt, 4 peppercorns, 1 bay leaf, 1 crushed garlic,
¼ teaspoon thyme, ¼ teaspoon tarragon and a sprig
of parsley. Simmer until just tender (about 8 minutes). Remove artichokes to bowl. Cook liquid
down and strain it over the vegetables. Chill
overnight.

*Heavenly Lemon Dessert   Coffee

LATE SUPPER

*Shrimp Gumbo with Rice
*Chocolate-Date Cake with Brandy Sauce   Coffee

LATE SUPPER

*Cassoulet
Tossed Green Salad
*Buche de Nöël

LATE SUPPER

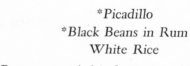

*Picadillo
*Black Beans in Rum
White Rice
Bananas sautéed in butter   *Rum Balls
Coffee

LATE SUPPER

*Clam-Stuffed Macaroni
Antipasto Salad

Escarole mixed with shredded Italian salami, chopped anchovy fillets, sliced black olives, sliced radishes,
chopped fresh basil or parsley, oil and garlic vinegar.

*Chocolate Ice Cream Cake   Coffee

LATE SUPPER MENU

*Russian Cabbage Soup
Cheese Blintzes   Coffee

LATE SUPPER MENU

*Paella
Green Salad
Crème de Menthe Alaska Pie   Coffee

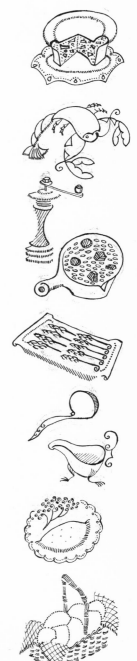

LATE SUPPER MENU

*Turkey Amandine
Chinese Noodles
*Raw Cranberry and Orange Relish
*Apricot-Macaroon Cake   Coffee

LATE SUPPER MENU

*Lasagne
Green Salad
*Peach Delight   Coffee

LUNCHEON

Cold canned madrilene: Mix with red caviar and serve
in cups, topped with sour cream
Lobster Béchamel in Patty Shells
Stuffed Beets
Belgian Endive and Tiny Tomatoes
Pears in Wine   *Fruit-Nut Bars*   Coffee

LUNCHEON

Spicy Tomato Soup
Quenelles de Veau with Mushroom-Madeira Sauce
Cold Rice and Pea Salad:
Cooked rice and cooked peas, mixed with chopped
parsley, chopped scallions, chopped dill, olive oil,
tarragon vinegar, salt and pepper. Chill and serve
on lettuce.
Roquefort Cheese Biscuits
Applesauce Tart   Coffee

LUNCHEON

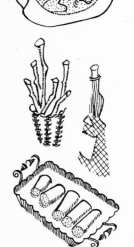

Cold Borscht in Glasses
Purée in blender 2 cans of julienne beets with
½ cup chopped cucumber, ¼ cup chopped shallots
or scallions, and 1 crushed clove of garlic. Mix with
2 tablespoons of sugar, 2 teaspoons salt, ¼ cup of
lemon juice, 1 cup of water and ½ pint of sour
cream. Chill. Put a spoonful of sour cream in
glasses. Pour borscht from a glass pitcher.
Caraway Cheese Straws
Chicken and Oyster Pie
Green Salad with grapefruit and avocado slices,
shredded coconut and French dressing
Puff Paste Mirlitons or Fudge-Brownies   Coffee

LUNCHEON

Chilled Artichokes:

Cook with water, oil, lemon juice, garlic and thyme. Serve with French dressing mixed with Bahamian mustard.

Baked Chicken Crêpes
Strawberry Lady Finger Cake   Coffee

LUNCHEON

Gazpacho Soup
Hot Coulibiac of Salmon and Lobster with Butter Sauce.
Pineapple Delight   Coffee

LUNCHEON

Mushroom Soup
Crab Quiche
Canned Artichoke Bottoms and cooked or canned Asparagus Tips arranged on lettuce with a vinaigrette dressing

To make dressing, mix French dressing with chopped parsley, chopped chives, chopped pickles and chopped hard-cooked egg.

Heavenly Apricot Dessert   Coffee

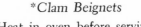

COCKTAIL PARTY, 4 TO 7 P. M.

*Clam Beignets
Heat in oven before serving.

*Chopped Liver
Thaw overnight. Chop again in morning. Serve with crackers.

*Cold Ratatouille
Thaw overnight. Serve with plates and forks.

Cold Marinated Shrimp
Can be boiled, frozen and thawed overnight. Marinate in French dressing, mixed with thyme and garlic.

*Cream Cheese and Smoked Salmon Dip
Thaw overnight. Serve with crackers.

Raw Cauliflower Flowerets and Cucumber Sticks
Served with Russian Dressing
Fix vegetables in morning and refrigerate in a bowl of ice cubes until needed.

Artichoke Hearts à la Grecque
Prepare day before and refrigerate.

*Hot Mushroom Hors d'oeuvres
Reheat before serving. Serve from chafing dish with plates and forks.

*Meat Balls in Barbecue Sauce
Reheat before serving. Serve from chafing dish with plates and forks.

*Quiche Lorraine
Bake before serving. Keep hot on a heating tray.

*Lobster Americaine
Bake before serving.

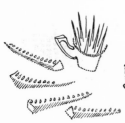

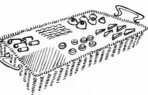

WINTER COCKTAIL-BUFFET FOR FIFTY

*Flageolet Salad

Use 4 pounds of beans. Finish preparation the day before and refrigerate overnight. Serve on lettuce with a garnish of canned tiny beets and artichoke hearts, marinated in French dressing.

*Pâté with Cognac

1 recipe. Finish preparation the day before. Thaw in refrigerator overnight. Serve with crackers.

*Broiled Stuffed Mushrooms

1 or 1½ times recipe.

Chopped Herring Salad

2 jars, 8 oz. each, in wine sauce, drained and chopped with 2 peeled and cored apples, 2 hard-cooked eggs and 1 red onion. Mix with 2 tablespoons chopped parsley, ¼ cup chopped almonds, ¼ cup red wine and ¼ teaspoon pepper. Serve with thin rye or pumpernickel bread.

*Lobster Béchamel en Croustade

4 times lobster recipe. Reheat before serving. 1½ times Puff Paste recipe. Bake in morning.

Roast Beef, Boned and rolled rib, or boneless sirloin—10 pounds
Roast in the morning, wrap in foil and keep in the covered roaster, unrefrigerated, until ready to slice. It will be juicier than if refrigerated.

*Barley Pilaf

3 times recipe. Bake in oven before serving.

Rye Bread

2 thin-sliced loaves from bakery.

Cole Slaw

1 head red and 2 heads white cabbage, shredded and mixed with French dressing, dill seed, caraway seed and a little mayonnaise.

*Individual Babas au Rhum, 2 times recipe   Coffee

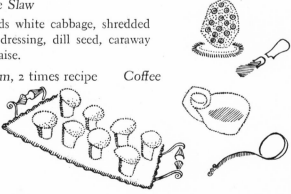

SUMMER COCKTAIL-BUFFET FOR FIFTY

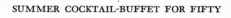

Cold Eggplant Hors·d'oeuvre:

3 eggplants, peeled and cut in chunks, parboiled and sautéed in oil for 4 minutes with 3 crushed garlic cloves, 3 chopped onions, 3 chopped celery stalks, 1 teaspoon thyme, 1 tablespoon soy sauce, salt and pepper. (Should be crunchy.) Chill. Make this the day before. Before serving, stir in ¼ cup lime juice and ½ cup olive oil. Sprinkle with chopped chives.

*Marinated Pepper with Anchovies

12 peppers. Mix with marinade day before.

*Cheese Ball with Crackers

1 recipe. Thaw in refrigerator overnight.

Cocktail Frankfurters

10 dozen. If frozen, thaw before cooking. Cook over charcoal grill. Serve with mustard, mixed with mayonnaise and tarragon vinegar.

*Cold Lobster Chunks with Sour Cream Dip

8 or 10 ½ pound lobster tails. 3 times dip recipe. Thaw lobster in refrigerator overnight. Make dip the day before.

*Cold Braised Beef in Aspic

About 12 pounds. Reheat and chill the day before.

*Quenelles de Poisson with Sauce Cardinal

Reheat quenelles and sauce before serving.

*Hot Black Beans

Bake before serving.

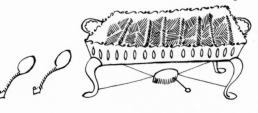

Lime Cucumber-Cheese Mold

Dissolve 3 packages lime flavored gelatin in 3 cups of boiling water. Add 3 tablespoons lemon juice, 1½ tablespoons tarragon vinegar, 3 teaspoons salt, ⅛ teaspoon pepper, and ¾ teaspoon dry mustard. Chill until slightly thickened. Stir in ¾ cup mayonnaise, 6 cups chopped cucumber, 6 tablespoons chopped onion, ¾ cup chopped green pepper and 3 cups drained and mashed cottage cheese. Blend well and pour into oiled 3-quart mold. Chill. Make the day before. Unmold 1 hour before serving, arrange on platter surrounded by watercress and tiny tomatoes. Refrigerate until ready to serve.

*Ice Bowl

Fill with cut-up fresh melons and berries mixed with mint sauce and use as a centerpiece.

Mint Sauce:

Boil together for 3 or 4 minutes, 1 cup water, 1 cup sugar, and ½ cup chopped fresh mint. Strain and chill. Can be frozen and thawed overnight in refrigerator.

*Fudge Brownies

3 times recipe. Thaw before serving.

*Raspberry Crescents

3 times recipe. Thaw before serving.

Hot or Iced Coffee

Make fresh regular-strength coffee. Have *coffee ice cubes available for iced coffee.

Note: My estimates of quantities needed for these buffet menus are generous, but I'd rather have too much than too little. Some things can go back in the freezer: the cake, the Barley Pilaf and the Lobster Béchamel, if it hasn't stood around too long. If the extra braised beef has been in the refrigerator, it can go back in the freezer.

Index

a

Amandine turkey 105
Antipasto salad 208
Apple,
    charlotte 156
    pie 159
    sauce, freezing 182
    sauce, tart 158
Apricot,
    cream filling for torte...........149
    dessert, heavenly 144
    macaroon cake 148
    meringue torte 148
    rum syrup 156
Artichokes à la Grecque.............207
    bottoms and asparagus
      tips vinaigrette 211
Asparagus salad 204
Aspic 19
    braised beef in wine............. 66
    with pate 27
Avgolemo, lamb 73

b

Baba au rhum.............................155
Barbecued pork slices................. 35
Barbecue sauce,
    for lamb................................ 71
    meat balls 35
    pork 35
Barley pilaf 126
Bavarian cream filling................165
Beans, baked 189
    black bean soup...................... 53
    black, with rum......................127
    cassoulet 86
    flageolet salad 33
Bechamel sauce for lobster..........118
Beef
    Boeuf Bourguignon 68
    Boeuf Stroganoff 70
    braised in wine, hot................ 67
    braised in wine aspic, cold.....66
    cabbage leaves, stuffed........... 89
    goulash, Hungarian 69
    meat balls 34
    Picadillo (Cuban hash)......... 90
    pie, steak and kidney............. 64
    pie with duchess potato........... 65
    roast 213
    stock 52
Beignets 24, 26
Beets, stuffed 126
Biscuits, roquefort cheese............. 48
Black bean soup......................... 53

Black beans with rum.................127
Blanquette of Veal..................... 82
Boeuf Bourguignon 68
Boeuf Stroganoff 70
Bombe, chocolate—coffee 168
    creme de menthe—chocolate..170
Borscht, cold 210
Bouillabaisse 60
Brandy cream sauce....................152
Braised beef in wine..............66, 67
Braised duck with cherries.........107
Bread 42-50
    croutons 186
    crumbs 186
Bread, quick,
    biscuits, Roquefort cheese....... 48
    garlic 50
    herb 49
    onion 49
Bread, yeast,
    cheese 42
    herb spiral 44
    muffins, toasted almond........... 48
    on freezing 50
    onion rolls 47
    tomato juice 46
Breast of chicken,
    to slice thinly.......................188
    with grapes, see Supreme de
      volaille veronique 97
    Italian style, see Petti
      di pollo Lombardy.............. 98
    and oyster pie...................... 98
    stuffed, in pastry crust.............100
Broccoli mold with almonds........128
Broth, beef, see stock.............. 52
    chicken, see stock.................. 52
    freezing 188
Brown sauce 194
Buche de Noel...........................150
Butter 184, 185
    lobster 115
    sauce 112

c

Cabbage leaves, stuffed............. 89
Cabbage soup, Russian............... 54
Cake,
    apricot-macaroon 148
    baba au rhum........................155
    buche de Noel.......................150
    cheese 154
    chocolate-date 152
    chocolate ice cream................175

Cake,
   chocolate mousse lady finger....147
   crumbs, freezing 187
   freezing 182
   pineapple lady finger.................146
   prune 153
   strawberry ice cream................174
   strawberry lady finger................145
Canapes, freezing 187
   cheese, caraway 29
Caraway cheese canapes................ 29
   cheese straws 30
Cardinal sauce 115
Cassoulet 86
Celeri remoulade 204
Centerpiece, decorative ice bowl..198
Charlotte, apple 156
Cheddar cheese bread................. 42
Cheese,
   biscuits roquefort 48
   bread 42
   cake 154
   canapes, caraway 29
   curried ball or slices................ 30
   freezing 184
   grated, freezing 185
   mold, lime cucumber..............215
   pie, see Quiche Lorraine.......... 31
   rolls, potato 135
   Roquefort, freezing 185
   sauce for crepes.......................102
   Spanakopetes (Greek
     spinach-cheese triangles) 32
   straws, caraway 30
   turnovers 28
   zucchini mousse au gratin........140
Cherry crescent 162
Chestnut (s),
   braised 129
   freezing 196
   puree in orange cups................129
Chicken,
   breasts, in pastry crust..............100
   breasts, Italian style, see Petti
     di Pollo Lombardy................ 98
   coq au vin................................. 95
   crepes 102
   frozen raw, thawing.................. 18
   giblets, freezing 188
   chicken-kumquat 96
   and oyster pie........................... 98
   -liver beignets 26
   liver, chopped 26
   liver, freezing 188
   liver pate 27
   liver sauce 195

Chicken,
   liver turnover 28
   paella 104
   paprika 94
   petti di pollo Lombardy.......... 98
   poulet a la Vallee d'Auge........ 93
   roast, freezing 108
   salad 105
   stock 52
   supreme de volaille veronique.. 97
   and sweetbreads, Suisse............ 92
   tarragon with mushrooms........ 94
   in wine, see coq au vin............ 95
Chinese,
   barbecued pork slices............. 35
   dinner 206
   fish ball and watercress soup....206
   fried rice 138
   fried shrimp balls..................... 37
   noodles, freezing 189
   roast duck 206
   spareribs with kumquats.......... 85
   spicy sauce 37
   sweet and sour pork............... 84
Chocolate,
   bombe, creme de menthe........170
   bombe, pistachio 170
   see also buche de noel.............150
   -coffee bombe 168
   colettes, parfait-filled 173
   -date cake 152
   dessert, frozen orange
     cream 176
   freezing 200
   fudge brownies 163
   fudge icing 175
   ice cream cake.........................175
   -mint sauce 165
   mousse 168
   mousse lady finger cake...........147
   -rum bavarian cream filling........165
   rum sauce, hot...........................166
Clam,
   beignets 24
   broth puffs 24
   filling for puffs......................... 25
   -stuffed macaroni 132
Cocktail tidbits, freezing.............200
Coconut, grated 195
   milk 195
   snowballs 199
   toasted 195
Coffee,
   bombe, chocolate 168
   freezing 200
   ice cubes 197

Coffee,
 -Kalhua mousse 163
Cole slaw 213
Colettes, parfait-filled chocolate....173
Coq au vin............................... 95
Cookies,
  crescents, raspberry or cherry....162
  crumbs, freezing 187
  freezing 182
  fruit-nut bars 161
  fudge brownies 163
  puff paste mirlitons...................181
  puff paste stars..........................180
  rum balls 162
  turnovers, currant-filled 182
Cooling 15
Cornmeal, see polenta.................135
Coulibiac of salmon and lobster..110
Crabmeat,
  bisque 59
  shellfish croquettes 36
  devilled 38
  filling for puffs.......................... 25
  quiche 122
  gumbo, shrimp and..................123
  seafood crepe pie.....................120
Cranberry (s),
  cream 192
  -orange relish 193
  pie garnish 192
  raw, freezing 192
Cream, freezing 185
  whipped cream mounds......54-186
  whipped cream filling for
    cream puffs 164
  cream puff pyramid, see
    croquembouche 166
Cream puffs, see profiterolles......164
Creme de menthe—chocolate
  bombe 170
Crepes, chicken 102
Crepe pie, seafood........................120
Croquembouche 166
Croquettes, potato-cheese rolls....135
  shellfish 36
Croustades (puff paste)................179
Croutons, freezing 184
  sauteed garlic 186
  toasting 186
Cucumber boats 204
Cucumber-cheese lime mold........215
Cucumbers, Indian style..............207
Currant-filled turnovers 182
Curried cheese balls or slices........ 30
Curry dinner 207
Curry, Indian lamb...................... 76

Date cake, chocolate....................152
Dates, stuffed 177
Desserts 144-182
  apple charlotte 156
  apple pie 159
  apple sauce tart.........................158
  apricot-macaroon cake 148
  apricot-meringue torte 148
  baba au rhum...........................155
  cheese cake 154
  buche de Noel...........................150
  frozen chocolate-coffee bombe..168
  chocolate-date cake 152
  frozen chocolate ice
    cream cake 175
  chocolate mousse lady
    finger cake 147
  frozen creme de menthe
    alaska pie 167
  frozen creme de menthe-
    chocolate bombe 170
  cream puffs, see profiterolle......164
  croquembouche 166
  crescents, raspberry or cherry....162
  fruit-nut bars 161
  fudge brownies 163
  heavenly apricot 144
  heavenly lemon cream..............144
  frozen orange-cream chocolate..176
  parfait-filled chocolate colettes..173
  frozen peach delight................173
  peach pie, very high................160
  pears in wine............................177
  frozen pineapple delight..........171
  pineapple lady finger cake........146
  frozen pistachio and
    chocolate bombe 170
  profiterolles (cream puffs)......164
  prûne cake 153
  rum balls 162
  stuffed dates 177
  frozen strawberry delight.........172
  frozen strawberry ice
    cream cake 174
  strawberries in decorative
    ice bowl 198
  strawberry lady finger cake......145
Duck,
  braised with cherries...............107
  cassoulet 86
  roast, glazed with walnuts........106
  roast, Chinese style..................206
  tipsy duck 108
Duchess potatoes 66

e Eggplant,
    oregano 132
    parmesan 130
    stuffed 131
Eggs,
    egg white, hard-cooked............ 19
    whites, freezing 187
    yolks, freezing 186
    yolks—hard-cooked grated 186

f Fish—see also seafood, lobster,
    shrimp, mussels, crabmeat,
    clam, oyster 110–124
    bouillabaisse 60
    coulibiac of salmon and
      lobster 110
    freezing 124
    quenelles de poisson aux sauce
      cardinal (fish dumplings with
      lobster sauce).........................113
    raw, freezing 189
    soupe de poissons,
      Mediterranee 62
    stock 60, 62, 118, 124
    turban of sole, stuffed
      with salmon mousse...............116
Flageolet salad 33, 203, 213
Freezer 10
-cooked party 10, 11
Freezing, what to freeze................ 14
    what not to freeze 19
Fruit juice ice block or ring..........197
Fruit-nut bars 161
Fruit puree, freezing....................182
Fudge brownies 163
Fudge icing 175

g Gazpacho 56
Garlic bread 50
Gigot en Croute
    (leg of lamb in crust).............. 74
Glasses and plates, freezing..........200
Glazed roast duck with walnuts..106
Gnocchi, potato 136
Goulash, Hungarian 69
Gravy, freezing 188
Greek,
    dinner 206
    lamb avgolemo 73
    spanakopetes 32
Gumbo, shrimp and crab............123

h Hash, Cuban, see Picadillo.......... 90
Heating 11
    in casserole 15
    in double boiler...................... 16
    over direct heat....................... 16
Heavenly apricot dessert...............144

Heavenly lemon cream dessert....144
Herb bread, quick....................... 49
Herb spiral bread........................ 44
Herbs, freezing 20, 191
Herring salad, chopped...............213
Hollandaise sauce 195
Hors d'oeuvres
    24–40, 204, 205, 211, 212,213,214
    artichokes, chilled 211
    bean salad, white (see
      flageolet) 33
    caraway cheese canapes............. 29
    caraway-cheese straws 30
    celeri remoulade 204
    chicken liver beignets.............. 26
    chicken liver, chopped.............. 26
    clam beignets 24
    clam broth puffs...................... 24
    clam filling for puffs.............. 25
    cold eggplant 214
    crab, devilled 38
    crabmeat filling for puffs.......... 25
    cucumber boats 204
    curried cheese balls or slices.... 30
    eggplant caviar 205
    flageolet salad 33
    herring salad, chopped..............213
    lobster chunks with sour
      cream dip 38
    meat balls 34
    meat balls in barbecue sauce.... 34
    mushrooms, hot 40
    mushrooms, ham stuffed.......... 39
    pate, chicken liver................... 27
    peppers, marinated 40
    pork slices, oven-barbecued...... 35
    Quiche Lorraine 31
    shellfish croquettes 36
    shrimp balls, fried................... 37
    shrimp, marinated 212
    spanakopetes (Greek spinach
      cheese triangles) 32
    turnovers, hot, filled.............28, 29
Horseradish sherbet, frozen..........193
Hungarian goulash 69

i Ice,
    bowl, decorative 198
    bowl with fruit..........................215
    cubes 11
    cubes, extra, coffee or tea........197
    fruit juice block or ring............197
Ice cream,
    balls 199
    balls in decorative ice bowl....198
    cake, chocolate 175

Ice cream,
    cake, strawberry 174
    coconut snowballs 199
    creme de menthe alaska pie....167
    home-flavored 199
    parfaits 199
Indian lamb curry....................... 76
Italian,
    dinner 205
    lasagne 88
    osso buco 81
    petti di pollo Lombardy.......... 98
    risotto Milanese 138
    shrimp marinara 119
    veal rolls 79

Kidney pie, steak and 64
Kumquat-avocado lemon jello
    mold 207
Kumquat, chicken 96
Kumquat, spareribs with............. 85

Lady finger cake, chocolate
    mousse 147
Lady finger cake, pineapple..........146
Lady finger cake, strawberry........145
Lamb,
    avgolemo (Greek stew).......... 73
    curry, Indian 76
    gigot en croute (leg of
        lamb in crust)...................... 74
    leg, stuffed, with
        barbecue sauce 71
Lasagne 88
Leg of lamb, stuffed, with
    barbecue sauce 71
Leftovers 14, 19
Lemon cream dessert, heavenly....144
Lemons, juice, freezing................190
Lemon-jello mold with Kumquats
    and avocado 207
Lemon rind, freezing...................190
Lentil salad 204
Lime cucumber-cheese mold........215
Lobster,
    americaine 115
    in bechamel sauce....................118
    butter 115
    coulibiac of salmon and............110
    chunks with sour cream dip.... 38
    sauce 114
    sauce for seafood crepe pie......120
    seafood crepe pie......................120
    shellfish croquettes 36
    stock 118

Macaroni, clam-stuffed 132
Macaroon cake, apricot-...............148
Madeira sauce 194
Madrilene 210
Marinara, shrimp 119
Marshmallows 200
Meat, see also beef, lamb, veal,
    pork 29, 34, 35, 39, 64-90
    balls 34
    balls in barbecue sauce..............34
    balls, freezing 90
    broiled 18, 19
    cassoulet 86
    freezing 90
    frozen raw, cooking times....17, 18
    raw, freezing 17
    raw hamburger, packaging........ 18
    roast, sliced, freezing.............. 90
    to slice thinly...........................188
    steak and kidney pie.............. 64
    turnover 29
Menus 202–215
    buffet for 50 people........213–215
    cocktail party 212
    dinner 203–207
    late supper 208, 209
    luncheon 210, 211
    planning 202
Meringue for apricot meringue
    torte 148
Meringue for creme de menthe
    alaska pie 167
Milanese, risotto 138
Mint sauce 215
Mirlitons, puff paste....................181
Mousse,
    au gratin, zucchini....................140
    chocolate 168
    coffee 168
    creme de menthe.......................170
Muffins, toasted almond............. 48
Mushroom (s),
    barley pilaf 126
    caps, broiled 190
    freezing 184
    ham stuffed 39
    hot hors d'oeuvre..................... 40
    -madeira sauce 78
    raw, freezing 190
    sauce 194
    sauce, shrimp and....................117
    sauteed 190
    soup 55
    stuffed Florentine 134
Mussel soup 58
Mustard sauce 194

n Nuts,
  freezing 184, 196, 197
  bars, fruit- 161
  pilaf, rice- 139

o Onion bread, quick..................... 49
Onion rolls 47
Onions, freezing 184, 191, 200
Orange-cream chocolate dessert,
  frozen 176
Orange cups, chestnut puree in....129
Orange sauce, foamy..................176
Osso buco 81
Oyster pie, chicken and.............. 98

p Packaging, materials and
  methods 16, 17
Paella 104
Paprika, chicken 94
Parfaits 199
Party system 11
Pate, chicken liver....................... 27
Patty shells (puff paste)..............180
Pastry,
  cream puff dough,
    beignets 24, 26
    clam broth puffs................... 24
    croquembouche 166
  crust 164
    for coulibiac 110
    chicken and oyster pie.......... 98
    crumb 144
    for leg of lamb..................... 74
    nut-crumb 167
    steak and kidney pie............ 64
    stuffed chicken breasts..........100
  pie crust,
    apple charlotte 156
    apple pie 159
    apple sauce tart 158
    crabmeat quiche 122
    cranberry pie garnish............192
    peach pie 160
    quiche Lorraine 31
  puff paste 178
    croustades 179
    mirlitons 181
    patty shells 180
    stars 180
    turnovers, sweet 182
    turnovers, hors d'oeuvre........... 28
Paupiettes de veau (stuffed
  veal rolls) 80
Pea puree, stuffing for zucchini..142
Pears in wine............................177
Peppers, freezing 184, 190

Peppers, marinated 40
Petti di pollo Lombardy (chicken
  breasts, Italian style)................ 98
Picadillo (Cuban hash)................ 90
Pie,
  apple 159
  apple charlotte.......................156
  applesauce tart 158
  chicken and oyster.................. 98
  creme de menthe alaska............167
  crabmeat quiche 122
  freezing 182
  garnish, cranberry 192
  peach 160
  quiche Lorraine 31
  seafood crepe 120
  steak and kidney..................... 64
Pea soup, fresh green.................. 54
Peach
  delight, frozen 173
  pie, very high..........................160
  sauce 173
Pilaf,
  barley 126
  rice-nut 139
Pimientos, freezing 200
Pineapple,
  delight, frozen 171
  lady-finger cake 146
Polenta, baked 135
Pork,
  barbecued pork slices............... 35
  Chinese spareribs with
    kumquats 85
  sweet and sour......................... 84
Potato (s),
  baked stuffed 189
  cheese rolls 135
  duchess 66
  gnocchi 136
  how not to freeze..................... 19
  and leek soup
    (see vichyssoise) 58
  mashed 189
  pancakes 189
Poulet a la vallee d'Auge............ 93
Poultry 92–108, 206
Prune cake 153
Profiterolles (cream puffs)..........164
Puffs, clam broth....................... 24
Puff paste 178

q Quantity preparation, cooking...... 20
  menus 21, 213–215
  packaging 20
  reheating 21

Quenelles de poisson aux sauce cardinal (fish dumplings with lobster sauce) 113
Quenelles de Veau with mushroom-madeira sauce (veal dumplings) 77
Quiche, crabmeat 122
Quiche Lorraine........................... 31
Quick-freezing 16

Raspberry crescents 162
Ratatouille 137
Rice,
    fried 138
    green, stuffing for zucchini......141
    how not to freeze..................... 19
    -nut pilaf 139
    paella 104
    and pea salad, cold.................210
    pilaf with chick peas...............206
    risotto Milanese 138
    white 207
Rum balls 162
Risotto Milanese 138
Rolls, onion 47
Russian cabbage soup.................... 54

Salad,
    antipasto 208
    artichoke bottoms and asparagus tips vinaigrette......211
    asparagus 204
    chicken 105
    cold rice and pea.....................210
    flageolet 33
    green bean 206
    in decorative ice bowl..............198
    ingredients 15, 19
    lentil 204
    preparation 11
    spinach 205
Salmon and lobster, coulibiac of..110
Salmon mousse, turban of sole, stuffed with 116
Sauce,
    barbecue for lamb..................... 71
        meat balls........................... 35
        pork 35
    bechamel for lobster................118
    brandy cream 152
    brown 194
    brown, quick 78
    butter 112
    cardinal (lobster) 114
    cheese sauce for crepes.............102
    chicken-liver 195
    Chinese spicy 37

Sauce,
    chocolate mint 165
    chocolate rum, hot..................166
    foamy orange 176
    hollandaise 195
    lobster for seafood crepe pie....120
    madeira 194
    mint 215
    mushroom-madeira 78
    mushroom 194
    mustard 194
    peach 173
    red wine 194
    shrimp-mushroom 117
    sour cream dip........................ 39
    spaghetti, freezing 90
    strawberry 172
Scallopine of veal with chestnuts.. 83
Seafood,
    clam beignets 24
    clam broth puffs...................... 24
    clam filling for puffs.............. 25
    clam stuffing for macaroni......132
    coulibiac of salmon and lobster 110
    crab, devilled 38
    crabmeat bisque 59
    crabmeat filling for puffs........ 25
    crabmeat quiche 122
    crepe–pie 120
    freezing 124
    lobster americaine 115
    lobster in bechamel sauce........118
    lobster butter 115
    mussel soup 58
    paella 104
    sauce cardinal (lobster sauce)..114
    shellfish croquettes 36
    shrimp balls, fried................... 37
    shrimp and crab gumbo..........123
    shrimp marinara 119
    shrimp, marinated 212
    shrimp-mushroom sauce 117
    soupe de poissons Mediterranee (fish soup) 62
Shallots, freezing 191
Shellfish, croquettes 36
Shrimp,
    balls, fried 37
    and crab gumbo......................123
    marinara 119
    marinated 212
    -mushroom sauce 117
    seafood crepe pie....................120
Soft-ball stage, testing,................169

Sole, turban of, stuffed with
salmon mousse 116
Soup 52–62, 206, 210
borscht, cold 210
bouillabaisse 60
beef stock 52
black bean 53
cabbage, Russian 54
chicken stock 52
fish ball and watercress............206
crabmeat bisque 59
soupe de poissons Mediterranee,
(fish soup) 62
gazpacho 56
green pea, fresh...................... 54
madrilene 210
mushroom 55
mussel 58
Spanish, see gazpacho............... 56
spinach 57
tomato, spicy 56
vichyssoise 58
Sour cream dip............................ 39
Sour cream dressing....................203
Spaghetti meat sauce, freezing.... 90
Spanakopetes (Greek spinach-
cheese triangles) 32
Spareribs, Chinese
with kumquats 85
Spinach,
see broccoli mold......................128
soup 57
Florentine stuffing
for zucchini 140
Spanakopetes (Greek spinach-
cheese triangles) 32
stuffed mushrooms Florentine..134
Spiral bread, herb filled................ 44
Squash, see zucchini
Stars, puff paste............................180
Steak and kidney pie.................... 64
Stock, fish 60
freezing 184
Stockpiling 184–200
Storage time 18
Strawberry (ies),
in decorative ice bowl............198
ice cream cake..........................174
delight, frozen 172
glaze 174
lady finger cake..........................145
sauce 172
Stuffed beets...................................126
Stuffed eggplant............................131

Stuffed, mushrooms Florentine....134
Stuffing,
chicken for crepes...................102
clam for macaroni....................132
ham, for mushrooms................ 39
for lamb 71
Supreme de volaille Veronique
(boneless chicken breasts
with grapes) 97
Sweet and sour pork.................... 84
Sweetbreads, Suisse, chicken and.. 92

Tarragon chicken, with
mushrooms 94
Tart, applesauce 158
Tea ice cubes...............................197
Thawing 11, 15
Turnovers, currant-filled 182
Tipsy duck 108
Tomato paste, freezing...............200
Tomato soup, spicy...................... 56
Torte, apricot meringue...............148
Tomato juice bread...................... 46
Turban of sole, stuffed with
salmon mousse 116
Turkey amandine.........................105
Turkey, roast, freezing.................108
Turnover,
coulibiac of salmon and
lobster 110
cheese filled 28
chicken liver filled.................... 28
meat filled 29

Veal,
blanquette 82
dumplings, see Quenelles
de veau 77
Osso buco 81
Paupiettes de veau (stuffed
veal rolls) 80
Quenelles de veau with
mushroom-madeira sauce
(veal dumplings) 77
scallopine, with chestnuts........ 83
shanks, see osso buco............... 81
stew, see blanquette................. 82
stuffed rolls, Italian................. 79
Vegetables, see name of
vegetable 126–142
about freezing 20
fresh 14
purees 189
stew, see Ratatouille.............137

Vichyssoise 58

Vinaigrette dressing 211

W Walnuts, glaze for duck.................106

Wine sauce, red............................194

Z Zucchini,

mousse au gratin.......................140

stuffed, Florentine 140

stuffed with green rice............141

stuffed with pea puree..............142